Knowledge Nomads
and the
Nervously Employed

Knowledge Nomads
and the
Nervously Employed:

Workplace Change
&
Courageous Career Choices

Rich Feller and Judy Wichard

CAPS Press
CAPS PRESS An independent imprint of

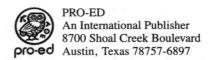

PRO-ED
An International Publisher
8700 Shoal Creek Boulevard
Austin, Texas 78757-6897

© 2005 by PRO-ED, Inc.
8700 Shoal Creek Boulevard
Austin, Texas 78757-6897
800/897-3202   Fax 800/397-7633
www.proedinc.com

ISBN 1-4164-0062-1 (Previously CAPS ISBN 1-56109-111-1)

This book was developed and produced by CAPS Press, formerly
associated with ERIC/CASS, and creator of many titles for the
counseling, assessment, and educational fields. In 2004, CAPS Press
became an independent imprint of PRO-ED, Inc.

Printed in the United States of America

1   2   3   4   5   6   7   8   9   10   08   07   06   05   04

Knowledge Nomads and the Nervously Employed:

WORKPLACE CHANGE & COURAGEOUS CAREER CHOICES

Preface

As editors and publishers, we find that the manuscripts we receive can be sorted into two categories: 1) those that offer insights into broad, societal conditions and the cultural milieu affecting human behavior; and 2) those whose primary aim is to provide guidance in implementing viable counselor interventions. This book is unique in that Rich Feller and Judy Whichard, with a compelling passion and excitement, do both. They provide an insightful look into life and the world of work as we know it today. Further, they describe what knowledge and behaviors people need to adopt to avoid being "nervously employed" – wondering whether or when they might become unemployed or unemployable.

It is a rare combination of a sage overview of the real world and practical, usable actions for acquiring some of the skills and behaviors of the "knowledge nomad" and getting on with life in a world of challenge and change. Unlike many of the manuscripts we receive which leave the reader challenged or anxious, but no wiser as to what to do, this book will inspire readers to move out of the comfort zone and start making the *courageous choices* that we all must make if we are to adequately cope with the rapidly changing world of work.

A favorite part of the book for us is the final chapter where, in a remarkably concise and cogent manner, Rich and Judy synthesize the insights they have provided and then move to provide direct guidance as to the courageous questions we need to ask about the world around us and how we can play a role to better that world. Especially important, they ask us to examine ten cogent questions that each of us needs to ask ourselves in order to become more courageous in the career choices we make for ourselves.

A lot to do and accomplish in such a short book! That they did it so well is why we published it and strongly recommend that you read and act on it. We believe the world around you and *you* will be better for it.

Garry R. Walz, Ph.D., NCC
Jeanne C. Bleuer, Ph.D., NCC

Acknowledgements

Writing any book requires a great deal of agility, intuition, and a supportive community. Both authors approached this task with the goal of speaking from the heart about the chosen complex topics. Judy Whichard and Rich Feller, training and consulting colleagues for over ten years, combined their creative efforts in what became a rich, fulfilling collaboration. Rich, who loves to chase resources, present ideas, and envision possibilities, balanced and complemented Judy's love of words and written expression.

The authors are indebted to Garry Walz and Jeanne Bleuer for their encouragement, support, and faith in our endeavor. Their lifelong commitment to helping others find their written voice has influenced the counseling and career development field like few others. When they asked that we write...we knew it was time to get to work! Under the most difficult circumstances, they assisted us in completing this publication in record time. Without them and Counseling Outfitters, LLC, I don't know how we could have done it.

Judy acknowledges:
None of us ever accomplishes a goal without the support of others; and, as I reflect on the progression of this book, I recognize that I have had many supporters to whom I am unendingly grateful.

First, I want to thank my mother and father, who modeled the courage and tenacity I needed to complete this often overwhelming venture. To my husband, Phil, and my daughter, Lindsay - I owe you both a lifetime of thanks for your ongoing cheer leading, indulgence and personal sacrifices throughout my writing journey.

What can I say about my co-author and friend, Rich? You're the consummate "Knowledge Nomad"—thanks for helping me make courageous choices.

Finally, I want to thank all of those who unknowingly inspired my thinking—Robert Reich, Mark Satin, Martin Seligman, Harvey Hornstein, Alfie Kohn, Manuel Hinds, Max DePree, and the late Fred Rogers. When I throw my first global dinner party, you're at the top of my guest list!

To all of you noted, as well as all others too numerous to mention, I offer my profound and humble thanks. You've enriched my life immeasurably.

"I was successful because you believed in me."
Ulysses S. Grant

Rich acknowledges:

My work rewards me for interpreting how choices about learning, working, and living can affect others. Making meaning out of how change affects my family, graduate students at Colorado State University, and individuals and organizations with whom I consult has taught me much about strengths, intuition, and trying to be significant. Joy experienced along the way reminds me to pay gratitude to those who nurture passion, encourage potential, and demonstrate the courage to risk.

Barb and Chris give me my greatest meaning, warm my heart most, and create the richest memories. Because life is limited by time, they give me reason to live fully and without regret. Barb personifies unconditional love as she quilts a life of faith, humility, and service to others. Chris, our wonderful teenager, keeps me honest, reminds me "this is it," and is the future I hope to most encourage. While I dedicate my effort within this book to them, I hopefully validate their worth, promote their dreams, and walk with them on all adventures.

I thank the Feller, Falloon, and Cancilla families for believing in me, and winking when I stumble. From them I've learned that kinship is one's greatest wealth. May everyone meet Joe Vasos, Jack Kruger, and Pete Carner. Three better souls more gifted at helping other's shine I do not know. Victor McGuire, Gerry Paist, John Rath, Bruce Kremer, and Chris Kneeland, may you know how often you create access for others. Nat Kees, Grant Sherwood, Sharon Anderson, Laurie Carlson, and Rick Ginsberg at Colorado State University support individuality and flexible schedules, and I'm most grateful for letting me "check in." David Tiedeman, Bill Charland, Dick Bolles, Albert Ellis, Dan Pink, Tom Harrington, Arthur O'Shea, Robert Reich, H.B Gelatt, Mark Savickas, and my NCDA colleagues... you provide the material echoing in my voice. I hope I do justice in passing on your wisdom and spirit. Without Judy Whichard's many insights, integrity, and patience, no words would have reached these pages. Judy's warmth, wisdom, and wit can lead any horse to water... and make any project a great ride. To a most gifted writer and authentic friend, thank you for your generosity and commitment to globality.

Introduction

*"Career development **nurtures** passion, **identifies** potential, and **honors** courage in choice making."*

Rich Feller

Change and discovery shape the world around and within us. Dramatically impacted by sophisticated technologies and the choices created through globalization, the speed of change can surpass our ability to stay apace, throwing us into uncertainty and chaos. Increasingly complex opportunities and issues demand our attention at every turn. Consider the following:

- In the U.S., heightened productivity has rewarded capital investment rather than worker compensation (Mishel, Bernstein & Allegretto, 2004/05).
- Automation has dislocated workers on a scale not seen since the Industrial Revolution with "smart systems" gobbling up check-out clerk jobs at Home Depot and computer systems self diagnosing and repairing themselves (Lamb, 2004).
- Leaders have mortgaged America's future through reckless tax cuts, out-of-control spending, and Enron-style accounting in Congress (Peterson, 2004).
- Economic leaders are making statements like, "If we have promised more than our economy has the ability to deliver, as I fear we may have, we must recalibrate our public programs so that pending retirees have time to adjust through other changes. If we delay, the adjustments could be abrupt and painful" (Greenspan's Social Security Alarm, 2004).
- Americans spend 40 percent less time with their children today than in 1960, 72 minutes behind the wheel of a car daily, and a meager half-hour per week making love (Honoré, 2004).

This is the context within which the "Knowledge Nomads" and the "Nervously Employed" must make courageous choices during turbulent times (see Feller & Walz, 1997).

Think about how we traditionally defined "work"—shifts from 8 to 5; tenure at one company; wages to match our ages; specific job descriptions; up-the-ladder promotions; livable wages; retirement with pension at age 65; and so on. We felt secure and "in control" despite fewer choices and creative opportunities. As we fast-forward to the onset of the 21st centuries, we're met by a very different prevailing reality of "work". No longer "place-bound," "time-bound," or delimited by clearly prescribed job descriptions and products, highly creative, agile, and self-directed workers have evolved into "Knowledge Nomads"—workers possessing the skills and traits to continually innovate regardless of geographic location or time zone.

Sophisticated consumers across the globe demand excellence in their purchases. Their pursuit ratchets up the need for companies to continuously innovate to garner market share and capture the attention of harried and over-worked parents, technically savvy employees, and an indulged youth consumer culture (Feller, 2003b). With their capacity to work globally 24/7, "Knowledge Nomads" are in heightened demand, able to "add value" with intuition and agility anywhere and at any time. Their ability to maximize technology and negotiate databases surpasses the influences of time and geography as they produce and deliver on-demand excellence. And, as their name implies, these "Nomads" are increasingly loyal to their ideas, skill sets, and learning opportunities rather than to their temporary employer or company.

With their highly attuned radar scanning for the next available learning opportunity "and stretch assignment," these "Knowledge Nomads" elevate (or add to) the tension felt by their "Nervously Employed" colleagues. These equally important workers are frequently frustrated by rapidly changing expectations, accelerated rates of performance expectations, and frequent demands to retool. The "Nervously Employed" are the majority of employees hired to job descriptions that are no longer clear or definitive due to changing economic realities. Their positions and opportunities are fluid, yet these workers continue to seek job security.

The "Nervously Employed" are reluctantly coming to understand that there are only two kinds of workers—self-employed owners and "temps." They increasingly acknowledge that success and opportunity are tied to challenging old assumptions and making courageous choices about learning, working, and living. Take, for example, existing economic realities. Wages and employment opportunities have decreased for those U.S. labor workers creating products and increased for those providing services offering a human touch and/or systems thinking. Why? Technology replaces costly laborers, and temporary contract workers replace "tenured employees." Outsourcing accesses a world-wide labor pool. As jobs shift to countries that pay workers less, products cost less to create and can be offered less expensively to consumers. On the other hand, competitive services demand higher "human intervention," meaning higher wage costs for the added value and innovation attainable only through engaged workers. Consumers now generally pay less for products because they are probably made outside the U.S. and more for services because of the greater "human touch." The implication of these trends is that, to simply remain employed, workers must keep abreast of local, national, and global economic trends; develop and hone their skills and marketing strategies accordingly; and continuously scan for unique ways to create, innovate, and add value.

It is into such settings that career development professionals (i.e., career specialists, career and technical educators, organizational change agents, and educational leaders) must advise clients and students. We are challenged to help them both understand and negotiate these turbulent times and make choices that will bring them gainful employment and fulfilling lives. For *students,* we must help them understand that:

- The bar has been raised for achieving livable wages.
- Job security as their parents knew it is a thing of the past.
- All work is best understood as problems to be solved.
- Excellence comes from using one's strengths (which are not field-specific, but applicable in any work, role, or activity).
- What and when they study is more important than where they go to school.
- "Knowledge Nomads" are increasing in numbers, can be found world wide, and respond to the highest bidder.
- The "Nervously Employed" are increasing in number, are found world-wide, and compete against world wage scales.

For the *currently employed*, the messages are:

- Paternalistic company loyalty decreases as profits are determined more and more by a worker's ability to translate the timeliness and currency of what they know into added value.
- Job security decreases as the availability of world-wide cheaper labor becomes accessible.
- Employee loyalty is increasingly tied to organizational climate, the opportunity to learn new skills, and a sense of engagement.
- Gainful, fulfilling employment means demonstrating learning agility and "STAR" behaviors (see Chapter 5) on a daily basis.
- How one enhances or adds value to an organization is how one's contributions and benefits are judged.
- The "psychology of earning" ethic is challenging the "entitlement ethic."

Adults in transition must learn to:

- Expect change as normal and gain the emotional skills to manage ongoing transitions.
- Define themselves as more than their job title if they are to hold a healthy identity.
- Understand the paradox of relinquishing security to gain freedom.

- Recognize the trade-offs tied to both workaholism and balance.
- See themselves as consultants or "free agents" in charge of their own careers.

This book is meant as both a beacon of hope and a guide for making choices that result in successful careers, rich lives, and balanced perspectives. It is dedicated to all career professionals, educators, and organizational change agents who promote career development as an alignment of life-long learning, finding meaning in work, and living on purpose amidst the realities of a turbulent workplace. It's for those hoping that work is moving from a form of punishment to a place where people feel fulfilled at the end of the day.

We begin by presenting career development as the key under which all major life choices fall. Subsequent insights include workplace change, the new workplace skills, education reform efforts, initiating and propelling successful change, and the impact of globalization and technology on both work and global citizenry. Along the way, we offer implications for each of these trends. The ultimate goal is for readers to find the courage to make choices that nurture their passion and help them exceed their potential in all life roles. Throughout the book, we make an appeal to pursue a new social contract—one built on fairness and flexibility.

We are all chronically faced with competing demands on our time, prompting a myriad of over-whelming choices. Choices based on too much hype and too little germane information can cloud our search for life's vanishing simplicity and clarity. Our belief is that by focusing on more thoughtful questions we will find supreme opportunities for growth and fulfillment.

We live in exciting, yet anxious times as workplace changes affect how we live every aspect of our lives. By embracing a definition of career development that nurtures passion, identifies potential, and honors courageous choices, we can challenge our assumptions and find hope along our life pathway. Let's each make our journey with grace, courage, boundless dreams, and hope.

Knowledge Nomads and the Nervously Employed:

Workplace Change
&
Courageous Career Choices

Rich Feller and Judy Wichard

CHAPTER 1

Career Development As a Lifelong Lens

Career development is..."a straightforward process of understanding, exploring, and decision making, reflecting on your life, family, and work in a wider context. What complicates it is that careers and organizations are constantly changing. [Thus]... careers have been defined as a set of improvisations based on loose assumptions about the future."

Business: The Ultimate Resource (2000, p. 418)

Career development has traversed a long, sometimes circuitous path. Some career development efforts have been of enormous benefit to students and clients; from others we've learned more about what to do differently. In this beginning chapter, we visit career development's history, giving a brief overview of its most defining occurrences. We next discuss its current "holistic" models and their benefits to students and clients. The chapter ends with an overview of the most recent trends in career development.

Thinking about the evolution of career development is remarkably telling. Reviewing our recent past is most instructive. Over three decades ago, career development professionals were focusing on fitting clients into jobs or traditional dualistic learning options (college prep or vocational education) through mechanistic trait-factor approaches. While revolutionary at the time, the advent of portfolio careers, free agency, and downsizing have changed expectations about "jobs for life." We now know that matching people to jobs is much too narrow a perspective. John Krumboltz, a Stanford University professor holding an international reputation for theories on career choice and development, suggested in a 1994 presentation that, "...instead of taking people and matching them to a job, we need to help them determine career direction, overcome real and perceived obstacles, learn job search skills, avoid burnout, and prepare for new opportunities" (Simonsen, 1997, p. 205).

1

Over the next decade or so, the trait-factor approach or "fit models" recognized behavior modification methods and Job Clubs (Azrin and Besalel, 1980). In 1972, Richard Bolles' *What Color Is Your Parachute?* popularized and greatly expanded access to career development principles across the U.S. Skills analyses of past achievements helped clients break out of the "three boxes of life," and *Parachute*-related workshops paralleled an explosion of self-help books. Perceptions of careers, career development, and career development professionals were decidedly broadened, and expectations about their effects escalated.

Today finds all clients and students seeking strategies to help them develop their life roles *throughout* their lives. This places greater demands on career specialists, organizational change agents, and educational leaders to design and deliver "holistic career development" interventions and programs. Bowing to the growing complexity of career exploration, attainment and opportunities, new career development taxonomies integrating and balancing career, learning and life decisions have evolved (Dykeman, Herr, Ingram, Wood, Charles, & Pehrsson, 2001; National Career Development Guidelines, 1996; and Blueprint for Life/Work Design, n.d.). Moreover, people are changing in profoundly fundamental ways. Local, national and international crises—the *Challenger* explosion, shootings in schools, 9/11, the war on terrorism—have prompted self-reflection at the most basic of human levels. We've come to realize that career development, as all of life, includes a sense of tentativeness or "positive uncertainty" (Gelatt,1998), thus promoting renewed commitment to self-advocacy and self-management, heightened resiliency, and a clarion call to make meaning out of one's existence.

Career Development: Shaping the Journey of Students and Adults

Currently, we find that career development is a complex, dynamic field wherein specialists and leaders interchange freely the words "career interventions," "career assistance," "career counseling," "career planning," and "career coaching" as they propose and practice change models and techniques. It is increasingly accepted as a life-long strategy impacting not only individuals and organizations, but also national economies. When "...expressed in terms of measurable impacts on personal, community, economic and workforce development, [it] captures the attention of legislatures, policy makers and administrators" (Jarvis, Zielke and Cartwright, 2003, p. 269).

Potentially, career development fosters efficiency in the allocation and use of human resources, as well as promotes social equity by expanding educational and occupational access (Watts, Dartois, and Plant, 1986). As

2

examples, we now realize that the extent to which workers don't share in the success of their companies, live in poverty, and have difficulty accessing education are directly proportionate to their need for external support. Reich (2002) noted that those workers with the fewest opportunities for lasting and fulfilling employment need strong interventions from their companies and communities to not only achieve, but also to create career development plans to stem a widening income gap. When individuals, especially adults, are not readily malleable to changing work roles they "...will suffer transitional casualties: persons will be unable to work at levels compatible with their economic wants and demands. Depression, anxiety, and other mental disorders related to work will accelerate under such circumstances, and mental health professionals will be increasingly called upon to address career and work-related issues" (Lowman, 1996, p. 206).

Career development is also a socio-political activity that "...operates at the interface between personal and social needs, between individual aspirations and opportunity structures, between private and public identities...[Thus], the rationale for public funding for such services stems from their value to society and the economy, as well as to individuals" (Watts, 1996, p. 229.)

Although research illustrates its value, unfortunately, national support for more comprehensive career development planning is presently hampered by shifts in political priorities and mounting government deficits. Yet, as employers place more responsibility on workers for managing their careers, health care, and retirement options, career development has never been more important. For a comprehensive SWOT (strengths, weaknesses, opportunities, and threats) analysis of career counseling, please refer to the special issue of the *Career Development Quarterly*, "Career Counseling in the Next Decade" (Savickas, 2003), which commemorates the 90th anniversary of the National Career Development Association.

Why Career Development? Because It Works!

As we've mentioned, individuals, organizations, and government policy makers are not easily convinced that comprehensive career development planning is a sound investment, despite evidence that it works. In our efforts to learn about career development's benefits, we've uncovered a healthy body of research.

The Education, Social, and Economic Value of Informed and Considered Career Decisions (America's Career Resource Network Association [ACRNA], 2003) report synthesized much of the existing research and concluded that comprehensive career development leads to what they termed "...*informed and considered career decisions*" (Gillie & Gillie-Isenhour, 2003). Such decisions:

- Are linked to improved educational achievement, attainment and efficiency. Students who make informed and considered career decisions are more likely to graduate from high school and to succeed in postsecondary education.
- Reduce the likelihood of occupational mismatch and unemployment, increase the likelihood of career satisfaction, and result in lower incidences of work-related stress and depressions.
- Lead to higher incomes, fewer bouts and shorter durations of unemployment, better matches of person and work resulting in less turnover, better health for the employee and the employee's family, and fewer instances of work-related stress, depression and violence, which lead to savings in training, social welfare, criminal justice, and health-care costs.

Further, ensuring *informed and considered career decisions* maximizes the likelihood that *all learners*:

- Participate in education with a sense of its importance and relevance to future well-being;
- Formulate a flexible education and career plan prior to commencing high school;
- Have access to high quality career information and receive career guidance services in the context of a comprehensive school guidance program;
- Participate in a career development program that encourages students to engage in academic rigor and postsecondary education and training; and
- Learn the skills associated with career self-management that can be applied to career transitions throughout one's life.

Investments in career development ensure ultimately that *all workers:*

- Have the skills to cope with changing employers, occupations, and skill demands;
- Have confidence in their ability to advance and develop their careers;
- Understand the importance of fit between an individual and the person's work and work environment; and
- Have access to high quality career information and the services of career professionals who can assist with transitions.

The following chart presents the key educational, social, and economic benefits of career-development-based choices as summarized by America's

Career Resource Network Association (2003).

Educational	a) improved educational achievement b) improved preparation and participation in postsecondary education c) better articulation among education levels d) higher graduation and retention rates
Social	a) higher levels of worker satisfaction and career retention b) shorter paths to primary labor markets for young workers c) lower incidence of work-related stress and depression d) reduced likelihood of work-related violence
Economic	a) lower rates and shorter periods of unemployment b) lower costs of worker turnover c) lower incarceration and criminal justice costs d) increased worker productivity.

Career and Technical Education

Although not always viewed as a favorable "academic" option, career and technical education (CTE) continues to elicit positive results in high school students' career development and academic success. There is strong evidence that CTE reduces dropout rates by more fully engaging students in learning. In a 2001 study, Plank reported that, "...a middle-range integration of CTE and academic scheduling [three CTE credits to every four academic credits] has significant potential to reduce the likelihood of dropping out" (p. 35).

Plank's (2001) work also illuminated two important points about CTE. First, CTE is a particularly worthy consideration for students-at-risk; and second, the way CTE is designed and implemented is important to its success. Successful CTE is found almost always in schools with progressive, talented, and dedicated leadership. Further, effective CTE has two fundamental components—an upgraded academic core and a CTE major. An upgraded academic core refers to content and achievement standards comparable to college-prep or honors courses, including math, science, and English. The second component, the CTE major, requires four credits in a planned, coherent sequence of CTE courses supplemented by two related credits, including computer literacy skills. Additionally, those CTE programs that incorporate work-based learning further enhance students' educational, attitudinal, and employment outcomes (Bottoms & Presson, 2000; Wonacott, 2002a; Wonacott, 2002b).

Integrated CTE, defined as a "program" of sequential occupational courses integrated with a program of sequential academic courses, has the greatest appeal to students seeking sub-baccalaureate careers (Grubb, 1996). Integrated CTE has two types of goals: performance and outcome. Performance goals are achieved by mastering both general occupational competencies and academic curricula; the transition from high school to postsecondary pre-baccalaureate technical education or competitive employment is the outcome goal (Gray, 2002). CTE also fills an important niche; namely, it provides needed educational opportunities for the growing demand of technically-trained workers needing more than a high school education, but less than a four-year college degree.

Given its inherent focus on matching student career exploration interests with workplace needs, CTE continues to make a compelling impact on education's role in preparing the future workforce. As stated by Arthur Harkins (2002), "...CTE, with its technical focus and performance innovation outcomes mandates, is ideally positioned to lead the rest of education into new leadership and prominence" (p. 31).

School-to-Career

Few opportunities exist to learn job-specific skills within high schools. In many instances, secondary career-technical education has lost its power to move students directly to livable wage jobs. Without resources to expand high school career-technical education, it has too often become the preparation for individualized education plans for special needs students and potential dropouts. Yet, it continues to fashion an important legacy for all career development.

The School-to-Work Opportunities Act emerged from debates between vocational preparation advocates and college preparation purists that left students without basic skills and the potential to learn in context. Although the Act has run its course and funding has been terminated, researchers continue to unfold its impact to harvest important lessons. While the term school-to-career has hit hard times (it's now more "politically correct" to use work-based learning), the needs it tried to meet continue to exist. Past and ongoing research has found that school-to-work as a career development thrust had merit.

Hughes, Bailey and Karp (2002) report:

Our conclusion is that the research so far has found generally positive results: the school-to-work strategy does benefit students, teachers, and employers. Although critics of this educational approach feared that it would weaken academic achievement and divert students to low-skilled jobs, truncating their opportunities for college and further study, the growing body of evaluation work—even at the most rigorous and definitive levels—has turned up almost no evidence that such fears were justified (p.273).

After reviewing over one hundred studies, they concluded that school-to-work:

- Supports academic achievement in a variety of ways, such as reducing the dropout rate and increasing college enrollment;
- Teaches skills and abilities useful in careers and helps students think about and plan their future;
- Helps students mature and develop psychologically;
- Encourages more varied types of contact between students and adults, including teachers and work-site mentors; and
- Is viewed positively by teachers and employers (p. 277).

These findings are encouraging not only to school counselors, but also to other career development professionals and educational leaders advocating comprehensive career development. School-to-work/career strategies help close the gap among misaligned career expectations, academic expectations, and successful work behaviors by:

- Expanding higher-level, basic skills for all students and adults;
- Brokering access to occupational skills within high performance organizations that connect those learning about workplace behaviors to seasoned adult role models;
- Accelerating career exploration programs that help students and adults identify strengths and experience how interests can be tied to solving problems at work;
- Promoting "focused learning efforts" by using contextual learning as the springboard for building workplace talents;
- Expanding work-based learning through community partnerships so that students and adults can experience "real-life" success;
- Providing opportunities where learning is the constant and time is the variable, thus instilling passion for life-long learning; and

- Helping all future employees gain confidence about their futures.

Career Development: It's Not Just About Tests Anymore

To suggest that one can plan for a lifelong career by finding the perfect job is as naïve as thinking contemporary career development is driven by test administration. Yet, it has frequently been introduced to counselors-in-training as a mechanistic linear process of (a) meet and greet, (b) take charge of the process by administering an interest and personality test, (c) interpret results to find congruence tied to labor market availability, and (d) measure success by client clarity about what they "should do."

Now, we know that helping clients fashion comprehensive plans requires approaches well beyond individual "talk therapy." Workplace turbulence, pervasive (sometimes invasive) life style choices, and burgeoning appreciation for questions such as "What kind of person do I want to be?", "What am I doing with my life?", and "Am I living the way that I want to live?" beg managing career development creatively, spontaneously, actively and holistically. More often than not, work is an expression of deeply-valued purpose and meaning, particularly among clients without security and economic concerns. Many are no longer satisfied with working for a living, but instead want to work at living (Boyatzis, McKee, and Goleman, 2002).

Career Development: Enhancing the Journey

I think there is a "sweet spot" that each of us has…It's the kind of work we want to perform, the kind of work that makes us proud. But finding that sweet spot requires deep self-knowledge. You start by looking at the work you are drawn to. You try it, you evaluate the experience, and you evolve as you discover more about it. I think of this process as developmental self-interrogation. You're working on a mental model of yourself — always. Larry Smith (quoted in Warshaw, 1998, p. 138).

As career specialists and educational leaders, we are often in uncharted territory when guiding students and adults through career development planning. What do we — the professed "experts" — need to know? What questions might we ask? When do we ask them? How can we assist our clients in understanding and making constructive choices?

Career Development with Students: Promoting Its Use

Despite its importance in both career and life success, career planning is not a major component in students' education. Most students have little experience with comprehensive career guidance or computerized career planning systems. Those who do typically come from settings with more recently trained staff, significant technology support, integration of academic and career and technical education, and a high level of administrative commitment to a cohesive career development program. Most often, educational institutions provide student advising and placement services that seldom reach those students with the greatest information needs. *Decisions Without Direction: Career Guidance and Decision-Making Among American Youth* (Ferris State University, 2002) found that students perceive a lack of career guidance in their schools, and often cannot name anyone other than their parents who has influenced their career choices. Further, most admit that parental guidance is limited to a few hours over a few months. The study also identified a pervasive bias toward a four-year degree, ignoring those fields that need technically-trained employees even though only 28% of 25-29 year-olds obtain a bachelor's degree.

In an August 5, 2004, interview with *USA Today* reporter, Mary Beth Marklein (2004), about the book, *College Majors Handbook* (Fogg, Harrington, & Harrington, 2004), Paul Harrington states, "We've gone into this frenzy for kids in the middle and upper-middle class, there's almost a rat race to get into the best college. But the labor market is very good at finding smart, able people. The book says, 'Don't despair if your kid doesn't go to Harvard.' We also say too many students opt into major fields of study by default, without giving much consideration to their choice, at least with respect to the kinds of career options this choice will both create and eliminate. If you don't take the right set of courses in high school, it really cuts you out of certain occupations" (p. 20). Within their research that analyzes the actual jobs, earnings, and trends for graduates of 60 college majors, they find "little evidence to support the view that earning a degree from an elite college by itself markedly improves long term employment and earnings outcomes. After accounting for basic skills proficiency and undergraduate major field of study, graduates from elite colleges earn only 2 to 3 percent more over their working lives than graduates from nonelite colleges" (Marklein, p.20).

not higher Ed responsa

Most students entering career counseling begin with concerns such as, "I need to pick a college," or "I don't know what to major in." Typically, such concerns are often socially acceptable ways of saying, "I'm confused about who I am," "I'm nervous I won't find a place in the adult world," "I'm afraid of letting my parents down," or "I feel my worth is tied to achievement." Developmentally, this is "normal" - especially as most students experience little meaningful career development in schools, and most college courses offer little integration with career exploration experiences. Consequently, students often present problems needing imminent responses. Unfortunately, resolution usually means longer-term relationships beyond "quick fixes."

In the Preface to *Unfocused Kids: Helping Students to Focus on Their Education and Career Plans*, Garry Walz states: "...the issue of providing career guidance for all students is so pervasive and systemic that all appropriate educators and community members need to be enlisted to contribute to the effort" (Wakefield, Sage, Coy, & Palmer, 2004, p. xvii).

Career Development with Adults: Understanding Its Diversity

As individuals boldly attempt to integrate life roles, find balance, improve performance, and self-advocate for lifelong learning, they find that developing and managing their careers takes on greater value. Regardless of age and experience, following carefully crafted development plans is crucial since few individuals succeed in new roles by simply repeating past successful behaviors. "It is essential that employees understand the changing employment contract, hear a clear message about the requirements for success in the future, know clearly the business needs and competencies expected for contribution on the present job, and have the resources necessary for development in order to take ownership of their own careers and development" (Simonsen, 1997, p.196).

Adults, more so than students, understand the value of and want career planning assistance. Gallup Poll surveys found that nearly two-thirds of American adults would seek more information about career options if they were beginning careers anew. A 1999 survey reported that 42% of adults indicated that friends or relatives were their most frequent source for career help. An astounding 59% did not start their jobs or careers through conscious choice, although research indicates the critical importance of job satisfaction. Job satisfaction is the strongest predictor of longevity (better than a physician's ratings of physical functioning, use of tobacco, or even genetic inheritance, Palmore, 1969), as well as ongoing and future behaviors. "As a cognition, [job satisfaction] is linked to other cognitions, or cognitive constructs, such as self-esteem, job involvement, work alienation, organizational commitment, morale, and life satisfactions" (Dawis, 1984, p. 286). Additionally, job dissatisfaction is highly correlated with mental and physical problems including psychosomatic illnesses, depression, anxiety, worry, tension, impaired interpersonal relationships, coronary heart disease, alcoholism, drug abuse, and suicide.

Adults, typically responsible for multiple life roles, may see few degrees of freedom when they seek career counseling. Issues related to burnout and stress, transitions in relationships, sudden loss of employment, conflicts at work, poor communication with significant others, unrealized career goals or a sense of defeat are commonly interwoven with career

needs. Financial problems and care-giving responsibilities compe`
solutions and coping strategies rather than longer-range objectives, su`
satisfaction and meaning in daily experiences, defining success to match a
preferred lifestyle, or living intentionally based on clear priorities.

Numerous studies suggest that many workers are inadequately coping
with typical life problems, and need skill-building approaches that are
organized around specific life crises to better manage themselves (Herr,
Cramer and Niles, 2004). "For a growing number of people the real problem
lies not in a lack of job-specific skills, but in a surplus of social pathologies —
[there are] too many people with too little self-discipline, self-respect, and
basic education to fit easily into any workplace" (*Economist*, 1994, p.20).

Adult career counselors in workforce centers, private practice, or
within Employee Assistance Programs serve heterogeneous populations at
various life stages. Because of competing work-family priorities, career
counselors must often help clients develop what the Families and Work
Institute (Galinsky, 2003) calls a "dual-centric work-life." Galinsky (2003)
found that those who put equal priority on work and their personal/family
lives — who are dual-centric — have the highest ratings in feeling successful
at both work and home, with appreciably less stress overall.

Adults will increasingly face skill obsolescence, age discrimination,
and technological illiteracy. Seeking help in coping with feelings of loss,
incompetence, job change or voluntary or involuntary retirement is
becoming more and more commonplace. Early retirement, especially among
white males who prospered during the 1990's or worked for paternal
organizations providing lucrative pensions, as well as aging clients with
better health and longer life spans, may still want to work. Acting as
interpreters of "...lives in progress rather than as actuaries who count
interests and abilities" (Savickas, 1992, p. 338), the tasks of career counselors
include much more than working to help clients find a job that fits.

Career Development in Organizations:
Attracting and Keeping Talent

Organizations seek career development models when faced with the
challenge of attracting and keeping talented people (Pink, 2001). They
invest in employee development as a way to induce performance, maintain
bench strength, capture intellectual capital, foster innovation to drive patents,
and define or enhance organizational identity (Stewart, T., 2001).

Unfortunately, organizations are finding it increasingly difficult to
compete in the escalating war for talent. Career consultant Nicholas Lore
(Rockport Institute, 2003) reports that only "...approximately ten percent
of people report that they love their work." He does provide hope, however,
when he notes that, "...when fit is optimal, workers find numerous indicators

11

of increased job satisfaction, including experiencing work as a natural expression of one's talents and personality." In short, organizations need to find ways to effectively develop their human capital.

What does developing human capital entail? The most productive response seems to be dedication to developing people in three distinct ways: (a) presenting challenging tasks; (b) providing before, during, and after feedback; and (c) ongoing learning (Lombardo and Eichinger, (2002b). If organizations and their workers are to prosper, a culture encouraging workers to plan and assume responsibility for their career development must be actualized.

Career Development: Recent and Emerging Trends

Herman, Olivo, and Gioia (2003) state that, "...interest in career planning is at an all-time high and will become even stronger as we move into the future" (p. 108). Concurrently, they note that individuals, particularly younger ones, do not trust employers to control their careers and are seeking ways to manage independently their professional and personal development. This demand has given rise to a proliferation of career development opportunities and choices—computerized, video-enhanced, Internet-based, and curriculum-based instruction; eCareer Development programs within corporate websites; and career coaching, to cite just a few.

Career Coaching
Formerly provided only to executives, career coaching is now used at least as often as employee assistance programs or career counseling "...by managers and employees in a variety of work settings" (Chung and Gfroerer, 2003, p. 141). Defined as strategists in "...promoting continuous resilience and performance in persons and organizations...[career] coaches are often asked about personal evolving, succession planning, career shifting, work performance, high performance work teams, outplacement, burn-out, scenario building, leadership training, work-home balance, and individual and organizational renewal" (Hudson, 1999, p. 4).

Life coaching appears to use a solution-focused, results-oriented, systematic process driven by "...the assumption that clients are capable and not dysfunctional" (Grant, 2001, p 9), and what Hudson (1999) calls "experiential learning that results in future-oriented abilities" (p.6). Presently, there is little empirical research attesting to the effectiveness of coaching, an unregulated industry questioned by professionally-licensed counselors. With traces of consulting and counseling in the coaching background, as well as the application of contemporary management theory (Whitworth, Kimsey-House & Sandahl, 1998, p.xi), Coach University

(1999) suggests that career coaches are as much a part of life as per fitness trainers.

Career Development Facilitators

Responding to the need for career development training by staff other than professional career counselors, the National Career Development Association has implemented an advanced training program to develop Career Development Facilitators (CDFs). Designed for those working in diverse career development settings, this training prepares CDFs to serve as career group facilitators, job search trainers, career resource center coordinators, career coaches, career development case managers, intake interviewers, occupational and labor market information resource people, human resource career development coordinators, employment/placement specialists, or workforce development staff. CDFs are trained in career planning techniques and development strategies commonly included in most professional career counselor education programs. In fact, as noted by Chung and Gfroerer (2003), although career counselors, CDFs, and coaches may differ in their emphasis on practices as well as professional and ethical issues, many of the same career planning techniques and development strategies are used regardless of the helper's title.

Emotional Intelligence

Emotional intelligence (EI) is increasingly linked to success in school, family, and work life. Goldman (1995) states that, " EI is the ability to motivate oneself and persist in the face of frustrations, to control and delay gratification, to regulate one's moods, to empathize and to hope" (p. 34). His Emotional Competence Framework (1998), which includes Self-Awareness; Self Regulation, and Motivation as Personal Competence; and Empathy and Social Skills as Social Competence focuses career development professionals and human resource experts on identifying and cultivating competencies of high performance workers and workplaces (Dubois, 2002-03). Ground-breaking EI-based competency models, skills, and strengths lists are currently available and are being used successfully to enhance connections among lifelong learning, development plans, and improved performance.

Summary

Any lens that helps learners or clients see their choices more clearly is of great value. This is especially true in times of rapid change where agility and intuition are required for making needed decisions quickly. Reflection and thoughtful questions give room for new ways to reframe one's challenges. With career development taking on a more global perspective and our interest in searching for a new social contract based on fairness and flexibility, we are struck by four key questions proposed by Mark Satin in his work, *The Radical Middle* (2004). He asks:

- How can we give ourselves more choices in life?
- How can we give everyone a fair start in life?
- How can we maximize our potential as human beings?
- How can we be of use to the developing world?

(Satin, 2004, p. xi)

When answered comprehensively, intelligently, and honestly, these fundamental questions can move us toward enlightened self-awareness, immeasurable self-fulfillment, authentic happiness, and global citizenry.

Career development in its latest iterations is uniquely poised to help each of us achieve concrete answers and practical solutions to our fundamental life choices. "Many Americans are becoming increasingly capable and knowledgeable (and bored to tears at jobs that don't require initiative or allow for participation)" (Satin, 2004, p. 4). Encouraging probing, revealing self-reflection, career development helps us create and recreate our values and purposes, while setting and resetting life goals. It challenges us to accept responsibility for not only ourselves and immediate family, but also our larger world-wide family. It acknowledges that we are only as strong as our weakest link, and that achievement is worthwhile only when others have had equal opportunities and not been held back. Steeped in and influenced by politics and economics, both national and international, career development is the individual's catalyst for competing and living successfully in today's and tomorrow's world—a world responding to an emerging workplace shaped by globalization and technology enhancements and a multitude of choices.

Chapter Implications

- Career development has evolved into a holistic approach around which individuals create and live their lives.
- Career development has a growing presence in organizations promoting development cultures, giving and enhancing both corporate and individual purpose, meaning, and performance.
- Career development has become a sociopolitical instrument, infusing economic vitality into communities, etching humanistic values into workplaces, and enhancing personal freedom.
- Building comprehensive career development plans attends to the very personal emotional domain of individuals on their lifelong journeys, searching for satisfaction and quality in every choice.
- Helping create and achieve these life stories, professionals are in a wider range of settings with greater variety in titles and levels of training, and are consistently driven to keep pace with rapid changes.
- The only constant is that the number of individuals needing comprehensive career development plans will grow. This growth will spawn dynamic new counseling tools, strategies, and philosophies to help us help our clients achieve their desired potential.
- Career development is expanding from a focus on mechanistic matching of people to a list of existing choices to creating opportunities from things that don't presently exist.

CHAPTER 2

Globalization—It's a Small World After All

*"The broader challenge for the 21st century is to engineer
a new balance between market and society, one that will
continue to unleash the creative energies of private
entrepreneurship without eroding the social basis of
cooperation."*

Dani Rodrik, *Has Globalization Gone Too Far?* (2004, p. 85)

Globalization means many things. Many current arguments propose
and refute its very definition. It is a political buzzword and rallying point,
a chief consideration in economic predictions, and more often than not at
the top of corporate boardroom agendas. Increasingly, globalization sparks
hostile passion and contentious protests. Yet, regardless of what we think
and feel, experts agree on one thing—globalization is a present and future
reality. Most significantly, it continually impacts the very fabric of our
lives, our consumer options, and the worth of our labor. As such,
globalization is fundamentally important to conscientious career
development.

In this chapter, we introduce numerous understandings and definitions
of globalization. We speak to its influences on workplaces and worker
skills as well as its very controversial aspect of outsourcing. To help career
development professionals more effectively negotiate globalizations' and
outsourcings' complex dimensions, we provide a distillation of their key
aspects currently headlining political debates.

What is Globalization?

Globalization is intricately tied to technological communications,
economics, politics and governments. In fact, these words are often grouped
to define globalization—political economies, technological globalization,
international politics, international economies, and economic globalization
to cite a few (Bhagwati, 2004; Thurow, 1999). Contrary to how it seems,

globalization did not happen overnight; rather its etiology occurs shortly after World War II when Marshall Plan dollars were allocated to rebuild war-torn countries and restart capitalism. It was with the rapid growth of technology and its far-reaching telecommunication capabilities that globalization was catapulted to its current center stage position (Thurow, 1999).

Globalization reduces the time, location and shelf life of all competitive advantages. While globalization is not a new term, it is one that few families discuss over dinner although its impact is felt in nearly every aspect of their lives. Indeed, whether consciously understood or not, it is an underlying influence of most of their discussions—Walmart's lower prices, the travel schedule of their "Knowledge Nomad" relatives, fears about immigration, public education, and rumors of layoffs and downsizing.

Globalization can be explained through four examples—capital mobility, direct foreign investments, instant communication, and technology diffusion.

Capital Mobility:	Money moves around the globe 24/ 7, allowing us to get the best possible interest rates and venture capital to connect with any innovative, added- value idea regardless of location.
Direct Foreign Investments:	Because stock markets are accessible internationally, one never really knows who owns what company. Companies are bought and sold frequently, and with their branch offices across multiple counties in multiple towns, in multiple time zones, it is more often than not difficult to determine in which country a company ownership resides.
Instant Communication:	Through access to the World Wide Web, electronic communication can be in "real time".." Auctioned off to the highest bidders, satellites traveling around the globe report international events as they happen. Just as Desert Storm was broadcast

	live through CNN, any citizen with access to electronic communication experienced the "thrill of victory and the agony of defeat" at the same time as their Olympic athletes. If something is discovered at Colorado State University lab today, it can be downloaded in Beijing that night.
Technology Diffusion:	Technological tools can go anywhere that a literate user can take them. If one is techno- phobic, technologically illiterate, or unaware of the latest technological advance, they face an uncompromising "digital divide."

Generally, "economic globalization" refers to free trade, free capital flows, the diffusion and transfer of technology among producing and consuming countries/nations, international financial mechanisms, and financial trade regulations. In short, it involves all the dynamics that promote and facilitate the earning and exchange of fiscal resources. It integrates national economies into an international economy through trade, direct foreign investment (by corporations and multinationals), short-term capital flows, international flows of workers and humanity, as well as technology (Thurow, 1999).

Globalization is also defined by its influence on national governments. Because many international transactions are not regulated, global corporations by default wield considerable political and hence economic clout. Unfortunately, national governments that heretofore managed economic inequalities (e.g., trade restrictions, tariffs, wage controls) are no longer in the driver's seat. Consequently, there are growing economic disparities among countries, among firms, and among individuals. Returns on capital investment are up, while returns to labor are down; returns for skills are up, but down for unskilled laborers (Bhagwati, 2004; de Soto, 2000; Thurow, 1999).

While we tend to think of globalization in economic terms, it is much more than investment and trade—it's a social and cultural movement as well. It's a shift to a more connected world wherein barriers and borders are removed and changed; transportation and communication are more readily accessible; and people, goods and services move about freely. It has eroded historical borders by interweaving national economies and governments (e.g., the Euro currency and its multi-national governing authority). Humanitarian projects are coordinated globally (e.g., the "War on AIDS"), and work is carried out jointly across continents. Discoveries made in small laboratories are shared easily across time zones through highly sophisticated satellite systems. All this is leading to a highly integrated world of globality.

On a more tangible note, globalization offers organizations larger audiences for their goods and services. Local marketplaces are replaced by international marketplaces where a sale can occur virtually anywhere at anytime reached by technology and delivery systems. What this means for organizations is that the intensity of rapid change will escalate. Globalization places "…an even greater premium on rapid adaptation as a competitive advantage" (Hornstein, 2003, p. 8).

The Price of Progress

As with any vast transformation, there is a price to pay and trade-offs to be made. Outsourcing, the allocation of certain tasks to external firms, helps organizations focus its resources on a narrower range of tasks and specialized skills. This instills economies of scale rather than sprawling efforts attempting to cover all bases. Outsourcing is the current American employment tendency as well as its perceived malignancy. Growing numbers of American workers are displaced by cheaper world labor, creating local and national economic downturns and socio-political divisiveness.

Outsourcing to other countries is expected to escalate in the near and far future. Table 1 shows the number and types of jobs projected to move offshore to low-wage countries such as India, China, Mexico, and the Philippines. While some areas of work will be affected less than others, all will experience major shifts in employment location.

Table 1. Projected Number of U.S. Jobs by Type Moving to Other Countries*

	2005	2010	2015
Life Sciences	3,700	14,000	37,000
Legal	14,000	35,000	75,000
Art, Design	6,000	14,000	30,000
Management	37,000	118,000	288,000
Business Operations	61,000	162,000	348,000
Computer	109,000	277,000	473,000
Architecture	32,000	83,000	184,000
Sales	29,000	97,000	227,000
Office Support	29,000	97,000	227,000
Total	588,000	897,000	3,300,000

Note: To low-wage countries such as India, China, Mexico, and the Philippines.
Data: Business Week, (2003, p. 57)

To date, "blue-collar" positions in manufacturing have suffered the greatest declines in the U.S. to outsourcing to other countries. However, the number of "white-collar" positions outsourced has shown appreciable growth as well (Kirkegaard, 2003). Table 2 cites some of the largest U.S. companies moving "white-collar" work overseas. It is increasingly apparent that global wage competition and technological innovations will continue to influence U.S. companies' cost-saving measures and other competitive strategies.

Table 2. "White Collar" Work Moving Overseas

Company	Number of Workers and Country	Type of Work Moving
Accenture	5,000 in the Philippines by 2004	Accounting, software development, back-office work
Conseco	1,700 in India; 3 more centers planned	Insurance claim processing
Delta Air Lines	6,000 contract workers in India, Philippines	Airline reservations, customer service
Fluor	700 in the Philippines	Architectural blueprints
General	20,000 in India by year end (2003); big China research and development center	Finance, IT support, research and development for medical, lighting, and aircraft
HSBC	4,000 in China and India	Credit card and loan processing
Intel	3,000 in India by 2005	Chip design, tech support
Microsoft	500 in India, China by year end (2003)	Software design, customer support, accounting
Philips	700 Chinese engineers in China	Consumer electronics research and development
Proctor & Gamble	650 in Philippines, 150 in China	Tech support, accounting

Data: Business Week (2003, pp 56-57).

Undoubtedly the most telling reason for outsourcing is the dramatic difference in employee wages. Consider the following wage comparison and it's easy to understand why companies, encouraged by shareholders and consumers wanting Walmart's "lowest prices always" business model, turn to outsourcing to enhance productivity and reduce labor costs.

Worker's Average Hourly Wage

China	$1.00
Mexico	$2.38
United States	$21.33

(Montgomery & Palmer, 2004, April 4)

Although displaced workers and lost employment opportunities are the most frequently cited negative byproducts, outsourcing creates other challenges as well. Companies to which work and workers are outsourced lack any real employer-employee emotional connection, hence no allegiance or loyalty (Hornstein, 2003). Moreover, according to deSoto (2000), most countries with which the U.S. trades and outsources have not yet established the "invisible network of laws" that turns asset into capital; and healthy free markets will not develop until every country transforms from primarily informal, extralegal ownership to a formal, unified legal property system.

Certainly controversial, Lou Dobbs (2004) outlined his beliefs in *Exporting America*. Eschewing the economic benefits of outsourcing, denigrating the power of big business over national life, and denouncing corporate greed, Dobbs offers twelve outsourcing myths. We consolidated his views with those of Paul Samuelson (the Nobel Prize winning economist as noted by Lohr, 2004), Robert Reich (2002), Thomas Friedman (2003), and Thurow (1999) into a list of some of the questions behind current outsourcing debates. We present these questions to familiarize our readers with some of outsourcing's major points and their importance in career development discussions. When examining them, it is helpful to consider that self-interest is a strong motivation behind diverse viewpoints. For that reason we suggest that "how you see the show has a lot to do with where you sit in the theatre."

- Is outsourcing American jobs a natural byproduct of free trade?
- Is outsourcing good or bad for our economy?
- Although Americans are losing jobs in the short-term, will they will be better off in the long-term?
- Is it a fact that retraining workers who have lost their jobs, generally obtain jobs better than those they lost?

- Has outsourcing improved overall corporate growth in productivity?
- Has outsourcing created high-value jobs in America?
- Is outsourcing creating greater opportunities for prosperity in developing countries?
- Does outsourcing jobs to developing countries capitalize on productivity growth and educated workers not available in the U.S.?
- Is the primary reason for outsourcing to cut workers' wages?
- Does outsourcing follow proven economic principles that support capitalistic ideas?
- Do the advantages of international trade outweigh their loses?
- Can China and India close the innovation gap with the U.S.?

Undoubtedly, debates of outsourcing's virtues and vices will continue for some time, despite the widely held belief that not only is it here to stay, but also will actually expand over the next years. Resistance, change's escort, typically relinquishes its hold as more and more of the world accommodates and adapts outsourcing ideology and institutes its necessary infrastructures. Let's hope intellectual property rights, labor rights, and environmental considerations soon become more universally respected.

Closing Thoughts

As workplaces become more global and characterized by unprecedented technological change and mobility, competition crosses international borders. Speed and innovation hold key places in competitive success; and current and future workers are learning that "business-as-usual" means integrating cultural, social, legal, political, governmental, and economic differences when creating and marketing all products and services. More and more workers and the organizations with which they work are developing global identities.

In transformations of this magnitude, debates will abound as both winners and losers surface. While sometimes distressing and often laden with misleading or faulty information, healthy debates *should* be encouraged and probing questions asked. Educational leaders, change agents, and career specialists need to become better informed and do a better job of explaining in more "unbiased" terms the trade-offs of globalization. Only through a more balanced understanding can they address the very real fears and opportunities of the American citizens.

Individuals *must* accept change as "business as usual" and learn how to make frequent transitions from job to job. The "Nervously Employed" will need to understand the downward pressures on their wages, as well as the demand for continuously adding value through innovation and increasing productivity rates if they foresee maintaining high wages.

As the current shift from global competition to global alliances expands, the nationalities of major companies will become more and more difficult to identify. The rise of truly global corporations has opened new markets for goods and services and caused jobs to migrate to countries with cheaper labor. If these jobs were not allowed to migrate, economists believe that assembly-line employment would still decline in the U.S. due to the rise of automated manufacturing. On the other hand, globalization has opened doors for many "Knowledge Nomads" who can use their competitive advantage within the knowledge-based workplace to advance their "value proposition." With cyberspace as their home office, they compete in the larger worldwide marketplace and often are remunerated handsomely.

Certainly, risk abounds in globalization. Risk is natural when considering the magnitude of the implied changes. Cultural beliefs and values are in question; economic vitality and security are moving targets; few accepted international regulations exist; and new technology proliferates seemingly overnight—each in and of itself a major shift. In combination, they seem daunting. Yet, risk is critical to successful globalization; risk initiates "…the innovation, incentives and imagination that carry the world forward" (Yergin & Stanislaw, 2002, p. 417).

Chapter Implications

- Reduced and stagnant wages have less to do with lagging skills of American workers and more to do with globalization, technology-enhanced wealth creation, and deregulation.
- World wages increasingly are determining American salary schedules and employment opportunities.
- Employees and employers are more likely to see the career benefits of global integration and benefit from the upside of outsourcing when learning and working in situations where they are exposed to others from other countries.
- Work will be increasingly networked across international boundaries.
- Comparative values of goods and services will be evaluated on a worldwide basis.
- A growing share of economic output will reflect the combined efforts of multiple countries operating as a single, flexible global market.
- Time and space will be further compressed.

CHAPTER 3

Technology—Replacing Muscle With Brainpower

"Technology is like a muscle in the arm rather than a new arm...Its strength comes from knowing how to exercise it."

Rich Feller, Jefferson County Schools Keynote,
Lakewood, CO 9/21/04

No discussion of globalization would be complete without speaking to technology. Indeed, it's frequently hard to say which came first— globalization or technology. It's probably most accurate to state that globalization, while underway to some degree since early civilizations began trading, became manifest through technological advances. In this chapter, we discuss the various ways technology has impacted and will continue to impact our workplaces and worker skills. We present criteria by which to judge when technology might be used successfully to replace workers and when humans are irreplaceable. We'll address some of the implications of burgeoning technology on teaching and learning options; and what price workers,communities and societies are paying for technology's ascent.

Transformed Workplaces

Today, all facets of life are impacted by technologies such as microelectronics, computers, telecommunications, robotics, nanotechnology, and biotechnology. Genetic diseases no longer hold the same fears they once did. Plants and animals with altered characteristics are literally being created. Microelectronics spawned lasers, whose diverse uses include powering the telecommunications industry and facilitating eye surgery. Robots build cars that are managed by microchips. Nanotechnology will make most products lighter, stronger, cleaner, and less expensive and precision instruments more accurate. In short, technologies have infinitely multiplied connectivity among people for numerous purposes, making qualitative differences in everyday life.

Information technology, deregulation, and a global economy have dramatically impacted the nature of work. Fiber optics, satellites, and Pentium chips carry our most fundamental resources—our data, ideas, and knowledge. Computer literacy is becoming a basic skill for the vast majority of workers. Accessible in real-time, large databases now mean we have broad-based information available to inform our decision making.

Unfortunately, the current and projected need for highly skilled workers who can continuously add innovation to each process faces critical shortages. Many American CEOs and senior executives cite the lack of skilled workers and sufficient workforce training as the leading barriers to healthy, sustained growth. According to analyst Richard Judy of the Hudson Institute, 60 percent of the near-future jobs will require training that only 20 percent of present workers possess (Schaffner & Van Horn, 2003). Additionally, organizations are finding planning and forecasting mystifying—technologies change so rapidly they are uncertain about where and how future profits will be made (Thurow, 1999).

Technology: How and When Do We Use It?

Organizations, particularly the large multinational ones, have adapted remarkably well to the infusion of technology. In fact, technology has become so important to "the bottom line," that employing it maximally has become both an art and science. Hinds (2003) suggests that to acquire technology's full advantage organizations must employ *three key strategies*:

1. Coordinate complex activities horizontally. Rather than relying on the traditional "chain of command" where critical information is lost, include those individuals most closely associated and familiar with customer needs and desires.
2. Use technology profusely to expand the geographical scope of all coordination efforts. Create networks wherein everyone can "talk" to everyone else and share efforts and information.
3. Take full advantage of the networks in order to generate value added based on knowledge and logistics.

Their sophistication and seemingly inexhaustible uses have impelled organizations to evaluate when and where computers can replace people to increase productivity and thus enhance the bottom line. Levy and Murnane (2004) propose four key questions organizations should ask to help *determine the utility of computers*:

- What kinds of tasks do humans perform better than computers?
- What kinds of tasks do computers perform better than humans?
- In an increasingly computerized world, what well-paid work is left for people to do both now and in the future?
- How can people learn the skills to do this work? (p. 2)

Table 3. Analysis of Types of Tasks Performed by U.S. Labor Force

Expert thinking:	Solving problems for which there are no rule-based solutions. Examples include diagnosing the illness of a patient whose symptoms seem strange; creating a good tasting dish from fresh ingredients; repairing an auto with problems beyond computer diagnostics.	Computers can not replace humans; they can only serve as adjunct tools/resources
Complex communication:	Interacting with humans to acquire information, to explain it, or to persuade others of its implications. Examples include managers motivating coworkers; a biology teacher explaining cell division.	Computers can not replace humans; they can only serve as adjunct tools/ resources.
Routine cognitive tasks:	Mental tasks well described by logical rules. Examples include maintaining expense reports; filing customer information; evaluating mortgages.	Highly amenable to computerization.
Routine manual tasks:	Physical tasks that can be well described by rules. Examples include installing windshield wipers on automobile assembly lines; counting and packaging pills at a pharmaceutical company.	Prime candidates for computerization
Nonroutine manual tasks:	Physical tasks that cannot be well described by If-Then-Do rules. Examples include truck driving; cleaning buildings; designing and sewing dresses; setting gems.	Computerization would have little use.

(Levy & Murnane, 2004, pp 47-48)

They next analyzed and categorized the present and predicted tasks typically carried out by the U.S. labor force, ultimately recommending those categories that could and could not be successfully computerized. Table 3 is a synopsis of their findings. Their final advice regarding research and development efforts includes looking for changes in the tasks that comprise work to help forecast future jobs and skill needs.

The proliferation of computers has fundamentally altered the operation and coordination of firms and allowed technically literate workers to access information formerly guarded by hierarchical management models. Consider the following current workplace norms.

1. Workers can now inexpensively convey and consolidate information *quickly*, and this information can be made available to the field *in real time*. Extensive data gathering efforts and long delays usually at the top level are no longer necessary.
2. Computers and modern communications enable *coordination* of decisions from many people in different locations *in real time*.
3. Computers make it possible for enterprises to operate massively, yet produce individualized products similar to those of artisans.
4. Computers make information-rich databases such as Google available to all.

"These new opportunities have brought to center stage two aspects of business that were not very important in the industrial age: speed of reaction and creativity" (Hinds, 2003, p. 15).

The global economy and decentralized workplaces are being shaped by developments in both computer hardware and software, and electronic connectivity. For some time, larger organizations have been increasing efficiencies by standardizing and automating routine tasks. More recently, medium-sized companies have begun taking advantage of cheaper software and communications costs, maximizing advantages of the World Wide Web. The Internet's commercial opportunities and falling computer and communications hardware costs have created fertile environments for innovations that are creating new value and efficiencies for businesses of all sizes (U.S. Department of Commerce, 2003).

Nomadic Businesses

Where are current organizations located? Where will workplaces of the future be located? The answer is—everywhere and anywhere as long as they have the basic infrastructure.

Thornburg (2002) contends that businesses can relocate to any area with the following characteristics:

- Cheap and reliable bandwidth to enable them to coordinate far-reaching activities and enterprises
- An international airport to support physical mobility
- Access to a skilled workforce that can share and expand an organization's purpose
- A high-quality educational system (including a university or two) to provide highly skilled workers and support lifelong learning
- Nearby investment capital
- A high quality of life (i.e., cultural and recreational opportunities)

Once there, business will operate from a "dial locally, think globally" platform (p. 69).

Because the world-wide supply of technologically skilled workers is growing, businesses are finding relocating much easier and are thus more likely to do so. Much to the surprise of most U.S. employees, the U.S., once the country with the highest proportion of educated workers, now lags behind both China and India in the number of bachelor's degrees conferred (see Table 4).

Table 4. Globalization of Technology—Number of Natural-Science and Engineering College Graduates

	Bachelor's Degrees		Master's Degrees and Doctorates	
	1989	1999	1989	1999
China	127,000	322,000	19,000	41,000
India	165,000	251,000	64,000	63,000
Philippines	40,000	66,000	255	937
Mexico	32,000	57,000	340	63,000
U.S.	196,000	220,000	61,000	77,000

Data: Business Week, (2003, p. 56)

Transformed Education

Although typically not leading significant change or innovation, educational systems are incorporating more and more technology into their curricula. Technology and communications have enhanced and expanded access to learning opportunities at an unprecedented rate. The World Wide Web has brought resources to more people, creating partnerships where none were possible, and building networks that permeate traditional systems (Caine & Caine, 2001).

To equip workers with the necessary skills, schools of the 21st century must follow two main tenets: that learning is contextual; and school is a process, not a place (Thornburg, 2002). Interestingly, learning was largely contextual (e.g., stonemasons apprenticed to masters who taught their skills) until the industrial age gave rise to assembly lines—rote and repetitive jobs that demanded task segmentation. Unfortunately, the unexpected outcome was the creation of a generation of workers who adopted the "INMJ mentality." This perspective of "It's-Not-My-Job" decimated the collective brainpower of workers, rewarding conformity rather than innovation and creativity closest to the job function. Yet, at a time when current and future workers must understand that *everything* is highly contextual, a decontextualized approach remains *de rigueur* in most educational settings. The implications are clear: education *must* revamp its subject matter and teaching methods so that rigor and relevance are not competing goals.

Technology and Human Costs

All change is accompanied by intended and unintended outcomes, benefits and costs, as well as real and imagined joys and fears. Sweeping technological changes are certainly a case in point, particularly when we observe their human toll. "Profound technological advances, while opening the road for a better future in the long run, are terribly disruptive in the short term" (Hinds, 2003, p. xvii). People who once believed their futures were a continuation of the past suddenly find their skills obsolete, replaced by new technologies or lifestyles issues accompanying them. Activities that were once economic mainstays have become unprofitable seemingly overnight either because their value disappeared or the manufacture of their products relocated to another part of the world. Across America, we're experiencing numerous economic and social disruptions, including unemployment, unequal distribution of income, bankruptcies, financial crises, and depression. Life for some has become unbearably unstable, the future agonizingly uncertain (Heet, 2004; Hinds, 2003; Jeserich & Toft, 2004).

The rapid technological transformation disrupts the foundations of our social life. Those linkages that provide order and meaning in our relationships and give shape to society are shifting, posing challenges to stability. Disruptions this strong elicit resistance that can lead to chaos, violence and an imposed, aggressive authority that escalates rather than ameliorates underlying tension and fear. As a result, societal disorder reigns and hampers all human efforts to adapt and progress.

Technological change also provides unparalleled opportunities for meaningful learning, as long as we ask and answer the right kinds of questions. Hinds (2003) proposes that now is the time to debate the following issues. Perhaps through our quest to answer such questions, we can promote the benefits of technology, while healing those affected adversely.

- What makes the difference between those societies that react positively to technological changes, creating a superior social order from them and those that react negatively to them, generating in the process revolutions and destructive regimes?
- What are the policies that governments and societies can adopt to ease the transition toward the more humane and efficient society that technology and connectivity are offering, avoiding a repetition of the destruction caused by the tragic events of the twentieth century? (p. xx)

Technology and heightened communication capabilities will play important roles in tomorrow's workplace, increasing the need for rapid innovation for organizational development and survival in the global marketplace. The emerging workplace faces assorted challenges as do owners and temporary workers who are asked to make meaningful choices about how, when, and where they will work.

Technology and the Delivery of Career Counseling Services

No discussion of the impact of technology on career development would be complete without examining its effects on the delivery of career counseling services. In two groundbreaking monographs, Bloom and Walz (2000, 2004) predict that "cybercounseling" is an emerging component of career counseling and not just a fad. They see it as an extension of the delivery system for counseling which all counselors and therapists can use to extend their reach and, in all probability, increase the efficacy of their services.

"Distance Counseling," a recent development in the delivery of career counseling and coaching services, makes use of several forms of technology, but relies primarily on the telephone as the most available and reliable form of technology. It has won the support of the National Board for Certified Counselors and the Center for Credentialing and Education as evidenced by the establishment of the Distance Credentialed Counselor (DCC) certification. A forthcoming publication, *Distance Counseling: A Handbook for Educators and Practitioners* (Walz, Miller, & Malone, in press), offers specifics on how counselors and coaches can utilize the new phenomenon. Because of the widespread availability of the telephone and the comfort level of persons talking confidentially on the phone, it is likely that distance counseling will become a regular component of career services offered by individuals and organizations. The newly established DCC credential will play an important role in identifying counselors who have earned certification as distance career counselors. Specialized training in distance counseling is now available from organizations such as ReadyMinds, Inc. (www.readyminds.com), which offers nationwide, onsite training workshops.

Chapter Implications

In this present and coming era, businesses will face the following conditions:

- Greater and greater *competition* will be coupled with more sophisticated and *demanding* customers.
- Demands by customers for *high quality* products and services that consistently meet or exceed high expectations will increase – there is increasingly less tolerance for defects at any level.
- There will be an increasing demand for *variety* in products and services.
- Larger markets will require *customized* products and services that must be delivered through flexible production to ensure profitability.
- Delivery of products and services must be *convenient* for the customer – customers will demand easy, friendly, seamless accessibility.
- Competing in a 24/7 global market will make *customization, service, and convenience* the only real advantages to shelf life.
- Armed with their technological arsenals, individuals – the only source of creativity – will be the crucial factor of production.
- Organizational success will be linked to innovations. Innovations create product differentiation, the singular most important element of competitive edge.
- Continuous learning will be required to keep any job that pays a livable wage.
- Those workers gaining in the present economy have attained marketable skills, have access to technology, and can create and convert knowledge into value added.
- The key to future economic security is not education alone; it is also a matter of being lifelong learners of strong character.
- What workers do today can be done anywhere in the world.
- Educational settings will experience significant upheaval as they initiate and implement changes in curricula and teaching methodologies.
- Career development specialists will need to acquire new skills in using technology to enhance their delivery of career counseling services.

"It's not the computerization that's important, then; it's the discipline you have to bring to your processes. You have to do your thinking before you computerize it or it simply doesn't work."

Peter Drucker, *Fortune*, January 12, 2004, p. 118

CHAPTER 4

The Triangle To Diamond Shaped Workplace:
Losing Security And Facing Freedom

"Success in these jobs doesn't depend on mastery of one uniform body of knowledge as measured by a single high-stakes standardized test. Instead, these new careers require an ability to learn on the job—to discover what needs to be known and to find and use it quickly. Some depend on creativity—an out-of-the-box thinking, originality, and flair. Others depend on the ability to listen and understand what other people are feeling and needing. Most require 'soft skills' like punctuality and courtesy (although some geeks succeed wildly without even these rudiments)."

Robert B. Reich *I'll Be Short* (2002, p. 73)

Anticipating and adapting to change has increasingly become a requirement for youth and adults to succeed at work. Companies are thinking differently, fostering cultures that encourage and nurture "…entrepreneurial values and attitudes that emphasize initiative and rapid response" (Yergin & Stanislaw, 2002, p. 407). Increasingly, the "new workplace" is more dynamic and less patient with workers unable to add value *quickly*. Responsibility for obtaining skills, training, and postsecondary education needed for employment has shifted to the employee. Global competition, technical advances and constant innovation continue to challenge employee tenure and vertical mobility. Workers are expected to be more competent in communication, math, computer technology, self-management, problem-solving, and decision-making skills. Employers who provide benefits are shifting from defined benefits to defined contributions.

This chapter begins with projected general demographic and employment trends in the U.S. workplace over the next few years. Next, we'll present the shift from the triangle to the diamond shaped workplace and the implications of this shift to employers, employees, and those seeking work. We discuss the impact of key variables such as global economic competition, increased connectivity, and demographic shifts on workers, education, and the workplace. We end by introducing a flow chart summarizing the key changes in the emerging workplace.

America's Shifting Workplace Trends

While opinions vary about the degree of workplace change Americans will encounter, the U.S. Department of Labor, Bureau of Labor Statistic's *Working in the 21st Century* (2002) lists the following general trends:

- The labor force is growing more slowly and is becoming older.
- More women are working today than in the past.
- Minorities are the fastest growing part of the labor force.
- Immigrants are found at the high and low ends of the education scale.
- Education pays.
- Some jobs with above-average earnings do not require a bachelor's degree, but most require substantial training.
- Workers with computer skills are in demand.
- The ten occupations to generate the most jobs range widely in their skill requirements.
- Benefits account for more than one-quarter of total compensation.
- Retirement plans are changing.
- Workers will be supporting more Social Security recipients.
- Years spent with an employer are down for men and up for women.
- The temporary help industry has grown dramatically.
- The most common alternative employment arrangement is an independent contractor.
- Most mothers work.
- Married couples are working longer.
- The workplace is becoming safer.

This report further *forecasts* that:

- One-third of the 30 jobs projected to grow the fastest this decade are in technology.
- One-half are in human health care.
- The rest are in education, fitness, and animal health care.
- Government, security, finance, and defense will continue to experience strong demand as well.

The list of *fastest-growing occupations* reflects the:

- Emergence of technology in virtually every area of life;
- Aging of the baby boom generation; and
- Increase in national security issues.

Recognizing the trends shaping the workplace, "… interest in career planning is at an all-time high and will become even stronger as we move into the future" (Herman et al., 2003, p. 108). Quite obviously, career specialists, educational leaders, and organizational change agents play an increasingly key role in motivating current and future workers to learn to be flexible and mobile, as well as to gain the academic, occupational, and career competencies necessary for success in employment and continuous development.

An Emerging Workplace Design: Triangle to Diamond

The rules of the global marketplace are transforming work, learning, and career development in provocative ways. Bill Charland, author of *Career Shifting: Starting Over in a Changing Economy* (1993) and one of our best teachers, created a new way to conceptualize the changing workplace. His creation of the pyramid to diamond shaped workplace led to further notions of an emerging workplace where "Knowledge Nomads" and the "Nervously Employed" would meet new expectations, new types of supervision and different responsibilities (Feller, 1997).

Traditionally, the triangle-shaped workplace (see Figure 1) honored and rewarded the top 15 percent of the workers—the professional-managerial class—or those who made the decisions, held the information, and exerted control. Work design was driven by engineers who removed responsibility and judgment from craft workers, farmers, and sole proprietors. Success was driven by efficiencies of higher volume at lower cost. Intelligence and talent were assumed to reside only at the top. Testing and sorting strategies served as gatekeepers to social and economic mobility. At the bottom 85 percent of the triangle, "blue collar" workers took direction,

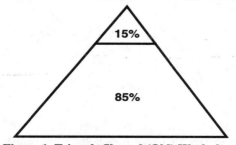

Figure 1. Triangle Shaped (Old) Workplace

followed orders, and were reinforced for "leaving their brains at the door." By meeting highly prescriptive job distinctions and stable skill requirements and following clear lines of authority, there were ample entry-points. During these times, beginning and low skilled workers, youth, and adults entered manufacturing, public utilities, and unions in great numbers.

Furthermore, North America's domination of the world economy and its competitive advantages led to significant job creation. Through seniority, collective bargaining, and continuous economic growth, workers earned more than average world wages. Management experienced parallel gains without asking for greater performance outcomes. This soon attracted competition from Japan and the "Asian Tigers." In the 1990s, the prohibitive cost of management's many layers and technology's capacity for "real time" information dissemination shattered assumptions about job security, the structure of work, and company loyalty, giving rise to a new social contract.

In the emerging diamond shaped model (see Figure 2) the workplace rewards employees with different skills, broader responsibilities, and greater flexibility with less supervision. Earning their value through meaningful contributions to a company's core competencies and mission rather than by accumulating degrees and titles, successful workers recognize the need to take responsibility for ongoing learning, risk taking, and developing requisite character traits. Workers striving to gain employment must have the technical skills, "intellectual capital," and personal strengths (Clifton & Anderson, 2002) critical to an organization's competitive advantage. Individual high performers are granted more flexibility, freedom and customized perks. Workers doing routine and repetitive tasks must be more compliant team players to stay employed.

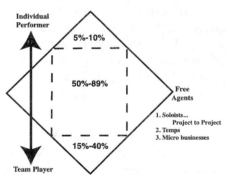

Figure2. Diamond Shaped (New) Workplace

Even in environments where it conventionally existed, job security is rapidly becoming an anachronism. State and local governments have outsourced functions, universities and community colleges have added significant numbers of part-time and adjunct faculty, and the military has altered plans for career officers and makes greater use of private vendors. Intense global competition as well as time-compressed distribution and product development have transformed work roles, job titles, and organizational structures. In the progressively global marketplace, the emerging diamond shaped workplace allows for fewer resources committed to managers or supervisors. Successful workers now assimilate traits of globally-competitive, high-performance organizations with less and less contact available to tele-workers. These elements include the following:

- Sustained market success (achievement of organizational objectives);
- Continuous improvement;
- Quality and customer satisfaction innovations;
- Product or service differentiation;
- Use of self-managed work teams;
- Clear links between training, development and organizational objectives; and
- Top-level administrative support for organizational and individual learning.

To respond effectively to changing workplace needs, workers need to understand that fewer entry-level, livable-wage jobs are available. Any inability to access and gain market-driven occupational proficiencies, retrieve and disperse information through technology, and remain motivated and self-directed handicaps all workers, particularly those starting out. Skills and competencies tied to adding value to an organization's core mission, increasingly determine the quality of jobs workers can expect to attain, their length of employment, and their opportunities to learn on the job. Moreover, current and future workers need to learn how economic fluctuations influence employment options, job growth, and job security; and how to access learning and skill development options during economic downturns. Table 5 contrasts the characteristics of the traditional triangle-shaped workplace with those of the emerging diamond-shaped workplace.)

Regarding job descriptions and tasks, the new workplace requires moving supervisory decision making and quality control tasks to all workers. Fewer primary, family-supporting wages, entry level jobs are available for students or low-skilled adults. These "Nervously Employed" workers are most vulnerable to automation and outsourcing. The fastest growing and economically most promising positions are technically integrated jobs requiring training beyond high school but less than a four year degree. Increasing numbers of college graduates end up without the credentials to get professional level or "core competency" jobs. Many have found it

Table 5. Characteristics of the Shift from the Old to New Workplace

Traditional Triangle-Shaped Workplace	Emerging Diamond-Shaped Workplace
Command control supervision	Supervision as "coaching"
Authority invested in supervisor	Authority delegated to workers
Centralized control	Decentralized control
Fragmentation/individual worker tasks	Work teams, multi-skilled workers
INMJ "It's not my job" view	Increased "dejobbing" view
Mass production	Flexible production
Long production runs	Customized production
Fixed automation	Flexible automation
End of line/process quality control	On line/within process quality control
Entitlement" ethic	"Psychology of earning" ethic
Company dependent career	"Own your own job, skills and career view"
Labor management as enemies	Labor management as allies
Minimal qualifications accepted	Screening for basic skills
Workers as a cost	Work force/talent as an investment
Internal labor market	Limited internal labor market
Advancement by seniority	Advancement by skill documentation
Information to decision makers	Information to all in real time
Minimal training for selected workers	Training essential for all
Narrow skills for some	Broader skills for all
Broad base of primary entry-level jobsLittle concern for foreign markets or labor	Fewer primary entry-level jobs Great attention to foreign markets markets and alliances
Easy access to primary labor market jobs	Previous experience, temporary employment, or occupational proficiencies before access to primary labor market job
Worker "classes" by title and degree	Workers appreciated by use of core skills to "add value" on a daily "prove it" basis

impossible to predict the earning power of a particular degree. Increasingly four-year college graduates do not replace two year technically trained graduates, they replace lesser educated retail/service workers, and low level manufacturers.

The unemployed and those with limited skills and resources face fewer opportunities at the base of the diamond. Those expecting job security or embracing the "entitlement ethic" face frustration, alienation and discouragement as they encounter change agents offering motivation and incentives for learning new skills. A colleague and employee of a large bureaucratic organization recently described his challenge of motivating "entitlement ethic" workers as similar to a "seasoned farmer trying to move rocks". He described the situation as follows, "...*entitled workers* often get their jobs because the job has to be done; while those employees who understand the *psychology of earning ethic* get their jobs because they are qualified to do the job at hand". This is a rather caustic, but realistic view of the inertia in bureaucratic organizations. At the same time bureaucratic and risk adverse organizations are "career killers" for those wanting but unable to create "stretch assignments" at the plant or office.

Within the diamond shaped configuration, many become empowered through creativity, freedom, flexibility and independence. Risk and entrepreneurship are welcomed, personal investment and self direction become a priority, and variable compensation rewards high performers. This often aligns with the values of the "Knowledge Nomad". At the far right and left points of the broad portion of the diamond, a number of "core employees" are of greater interest to employers as they possess the skills central to the companies' achievement and mission. Their work is less threatened by outsourcing or temporary contract labor.

Free agents (Pink, 2001) residing outside of organizations supply many of the skills closely tied to the organization's core competencies. As project to project soloists, "temps" or micro-businesses they identify and solve problems for project teams, organizations or the market and add just in time added value.

In our consulting work, we find numerous examples of formerly displaced employees of bureaucratic risk-adverse companies, invigorated within small start-ups that maximize individual creativity and innovation. However, not everyone can adapt easily. Those that can recognize that continuous learning and personal initiative are fundamental job requirements are more inclined to prosper and take on some of the identifying characteristics of the "Knowledge Nomad".

Transforming Career Development

Opportunities abound providing one knows how to access and use them. High-quality career development now requires that career development professionals understand the relationship among factors that create employment fulfillment and success. Figure 2 illustrates those influences and interactions impacting how learning and work is changing. Global economic integration and competition, technical innovation and satellite transmission, and demographic shifts are the primary driving forces in the evolving workplace.

The implications are vast, and lead to the need for a more flexible, integrated, and efficient "learning system" that serves more diverse learners in a wider variety of settings. Learners now want programs readily accessible and with flexible timing. Instruction (including career development) must also become increasingly learning style sensitive, customer friendly, technologically enhanced, competency based and partnership dependent.

As Figure 2 implies, the workplace is changing dramatically and rapidly. So, too, must our methods of instructional delivery and our instructional styles. Consider the following workplace and learning realities:

- The best jobs are filled by those who can manipulate math symbols, can scan and comprehend reading material quickly and write (communicate) persuasively and technically; are part engineer and part marketing specialist; are technically savvy; are those who see every challenge as a problem to be solved and have convincing intra and inter-personal skills that can attract followers.
- Opportunities to learn are everywhere. The obstacles of time and place no longer exist as learners can access educational opportunities anytime and anyplace.
- Teachers can no longer "own" content, nor compete with technology's appealing dissemination of information.
- Technological dissemination means that instruction is becoming more student-centered, encourages cooperative learning, stimulates (ironically) student/teacher interaction, and helps students take greater responsibility for their learning.
- Since information drives the workplace, the timeliness of a worker's information impacts their ability to add value. Accessing, evaluating and disseminating information via the internet provides unlimited "learning on demand" opportunities.
- Flexible, efficient, readily accessible and customer friendly learning environments are typically competency based.

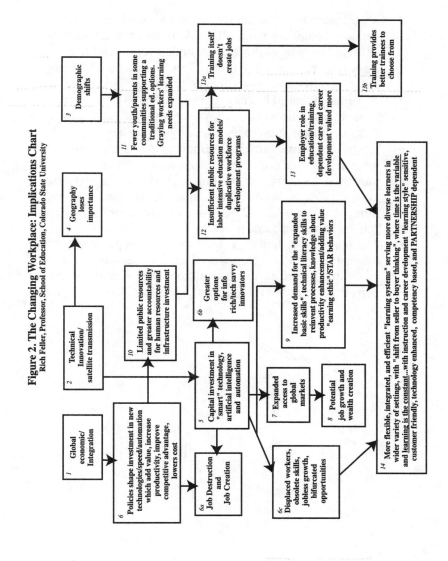

Figure 2. The Changing Workplace: Implications Chart
Rich Feller, Professor, School of Education, Colorado State University

Career development professionals now have many more variables to juggle when advising their clients and students. Fortunately, they also have many more learning options available to help their students and clients address the growing complexity of the workplace.

Chapter Implications

- A workplace based on innovation, speed, and independence demand behaviors from all workers that were formerly expected only from professional/managerial workers.
- Personal responsibility for learning and working autonomously are employment "givens".
- Technology-based learning opportunities will continue to expand; teaching workers how to access, use and evaluate them is fundamental to high-quality career development.
- Abstract systems thinking—employees making sense of what needs to be done, understanding how their work fits into broader efforts, and creating methods to "plug existing system holes"—is crucial to employee success.
- Supervision has moved from one of "overseer" to one of "coach" and "resource procurer".
- The majority of livable-wage jobs want employees with internship/apprenticeship/work-based backgrounds; proof of ability is tied to documentation of past and present performance rather than time in job titles.

CHAPTER 5

The New Breed Of Worker—Free Agents Tied To Cyberspace

"Knowledge Nomads offer high value, high performance, and increased productivity. Their "psychology of earning ethic" and lifelong learning commitment drive their success, agility is their password, optimism their mind set, and their goal is to agitate, create, and innovate "on-time, every time."

Rich Feller, Jefferson County Schools Keynote,
Lakewood, CO (September 21, 2004)

Knowledge has always been a crucial factor of production as well as a main force in economic development and wealth creation. Who has it, who can employ it, and who makes the most efficient use of it determine the rich and poor countries of the world (Hinds, 2003). Today, however, it is the *sine qua non* of organizational and individual success. Knowledge has replaced the foundations of past economies—land, gold, oil, and other such tangibles. For the first time in history, Bill Gates, the world's wealthiest man, owns the knowledge behind the production driving the knowledge and innovation economy.

We introduce with greater detail the "Knowledge Nomad" - the in-demand worker of the current and future workplace. We outline skills and traits inherent in the "Knowledge Nomad" and how they might best be acquired. Endorsing their findings on successful workers as analogous to our "Knowledge Nomad," we highlight Kelley's (1998) work on "STAR" behaviors and Pink's (1991) discussion of "free agency." It is our belief that, by engaging career development professionals in discussions of worker skills, their students and clients will receive the best possible guidance.

Knowledge—The Key Worker Asset

Knowledge today means power and privilege—it's the key to

innovative breakthroughs and economic success. It spawns groundbreaking technologies that foster the disequilibrium necessary for rapid growth. Knowledge makes it possible for traditional activities to be done in ways so different that old products essentially become new ones. Knowledge expands and enriches lives, broadens our scope of reality, and engenders clearer perceptions of truth.

Workers have been propelled (sometimes kicking and screaming) into this knowledge-based workplace at an alarmingly rapid rate. Yet, despite some initial "culture shock" and undoubtedly desperate moments, many have landed on their feet and are finding themselves enjoying their working lives to ever greater extents. These pioneers can serve as the role models for current and future workers where knowledge is the basis of wealth creation.

"Knowledge Nomads" - Global Pioneers

As curiosity motivated the American pioneers to fulfill their "Manifest Destiny," so too it compels the "Knowledge Nomads." Their curiosity translates into spirited "mental adventures," wondering why things work and asking how systems can continually improve. Gifted with foresight and the ability to multi-task, their ability to seek that which is "just over that next hill" has become their trademark. They're courageous explorers, blazing and traversing new trails. They're avid learners, getting new knowledge from anywhere, everywhere, and anyone. They're builders— continuously using new knowledge to create something different.

"Knowledge Nomads" are clearly aware of their employment opportunities, and they typically create their own opportunities within and beyond traditional organizations. With the requisite skills, they auction their work to the highest bidder and move from one project to another, leveraging expertise and compensation at the same time. They often move from one contract to another on a job-by-job basis, virtually impervious to the vicissitudes of employers or employer location.

"Knowledge Nomads": Works in Progress

Today's and tomorrow's workers need to learn radically different skills from their Industrial Age ancestors. Robert Reich, former Secretary of Labor in the Clinton administration, talked about the quality jobs of the future belonging to "symbolic analysts." His predictions have become reality. Successful workers are those who are able to identify and solve problems by manipulating images. Borrowing from Reich's (1992) "symbolic analysts," "Knowledge Nomads" grasp ideas and ponder their possibilities without the constraints of logic or emotional judgments. They experiment, take risks, ask "why not," openly share ideas with other specialists, attempt the seemingly impossible, pose the questions not asked, use the word "and" rather than the word "but," and strategically propose realistic innovative solutions. They use all available tools—technological and experiential—to create options and solve problems.

Daniel Pink (2001), in his breakthrough book, *Free Agent Nation: The Future of Working for Yourself*, was most instructive to our thinking about the basic assumptions of American work and life. We see the idea of the "Knowledge Nomad" as an extension of his very astute observations about the most prized, individually secure, and competitive workers who are able to adjust to workplace change. Their requisite cognitive skills (adapted from the writings of Hinds, 2003; Reich, 1992; and Thornburg, 2002) may appear complex at first blush, but experience shows they can be learned and individualized with great rewards. Their ability to do this repeatedly and at a faster rate separates them from those traits emulated by the "Nervously Employed."

Abilities of "Knowledge Nomads" include:

- *Abstraction*—This is the ability to discover and invent patterns and meanings from seemingly disparate, wide-ranging information. (As a note, this skill conflicts with traditional education and its focus on memorization of isolated facts.)
- *System thinking*—Following logically from abstraction, system thinking is the ability to think of most problems in the context of a complete system with interrelated elements.
- *Experimentation*—This is the ability to attempt something, note the results, and make necessary changes to achieve the desired outcome. An open mind, creativity, willingness to take calculated risks, courage, and spirit are all essential traits for experimentation. Growth, added value, and continuous improvement are always the goal.
- *Collaboration*—Working with others is critical as the majority of endeavors cross multiple disciplines and areas of expertise. Teamwork not only provides important insights in creative efforts, but its interactions provide feedback to approaches not discovered individually. Although technically not a "cognitive" skill, collaborating requires certain "mental" attributes such as *recognizing* when other perspectives are needed for an adequate outcome, *formulating* questions that should be addressed, and *synthesizing* diverse input without ego investment.

"Knowledge Nomads" are also identifiable by certain character traits. A "Knowledge Nomad" is likely to be:

- A contractor or internal project leader as opposed to a long-term employee working on routine processes and within repetitive patterns.
- Comfortable with ambiguity.
- A lifelong learner who enjoys intellectual stimulation.
- One who is able to "neutralize" the negativity associated with high-stress, pressure-riddled situations, turning stress to their advantage to maximize performance quality.
- Highly mobile and able to adapt to various situations, cultures, and languages.
- One who yearns for adventures that provide new insights and opportunities.
- Highly entrepreneurial, quickly understands the "value proposition," and sees most problems as personal competition.
- Thinks strategically to create practical solutions.

Contract Workers. "Knowledge Nomads" are part of a growing army of workers comfortable with the decimation of the lifetime employment contracts of past generations. They see themselves as consultants always moving toward freelance work. Their contracts vary in length, some as short as a day. They typically don't rely on company equipment—more often they are based out of their computers and electronic schedulers. Their loyalty is to their skills and, to a lesser degree, those who appreciate and invest in their skills. Bored by routine, they easily move from place to place, company to company, and on occasion from career to career as the excitement changes.

Comfort with Ambiguity. "Knowledge Nomads" understand that ambiguity is a "natural" outflow from the new working contracts. Embracing it is a survival skill, particularly with the rapidity of change causing uncertainty as to where businesses will earn profits.

Lifelong Learning. Although estimates vary, general consensus states that currently the total amount of information across the world doubles every two years. This exponential, inconceivable growth of knowledge makes lifelong learning essential for all present and future workers.

Neutralization of Stress. We typically associate stress with negative feelings and too much pressure. However, some workers thrive on pressure levels that would cause most others mental and physical paralysis. While stress tolerance is a highly individualized experience, "Knowledge Nomads" seem to reframe it in ways that provide internal motivation and maximal performance quality. They avoid the frenetic reaction that frequently compromises quality in the face of imposed deadlines. They are able to remain rational, and focused on the ultimate goal of innovation.

Mobility. The nature of short-term work means that workers, by necessity, are becoming increasingly mobile. "Knowledge Nomads" tied to cyberspace, travel from place to place meeting and conferring with different clients. Some may relocate completely and frequently without much notice. Technology makes them readily accessible. They use the web for virtually everything from paying bills to reviewing research databases, downloading music, shopping, and reading news services.

Yearning for Adventure. Although most of us perceive change as a threat, others feed off the stimulation of new places and random events. Stimulation, coupled with the desire to gain new perspectives and colleagues, compel "Knowledge Nomads" to travel to all parts of the globe—traversing time zones, oceans, and countries. In many ways, their theme appears to be, "S/he with the most experiences wins!"

Entrepreneurship and Creativity. "Knowledge Nomads" not only move from place to place, but also from career to career. Such lifestyles require them to be generalists, eschewing overspecializing so as not to loose their adaptability. Typically, they are quick studies, able students of the moment, spotting opportunities at every turn. In essence, they are knowledge entrepreneurs excited by the creativity behind possibilities. They seek freedom from oversight, distance from supervision and monitoring, and are adverse to bureaucracy. They're able to take their wealth of experience and apply it uniquely, bringing new life to old ideas and old ideas to new places. They trust their abilities and intuition, take pride in their creations and agility, are motivated by a desire for innovation and self expression, are adventurous risk-takers, and are willing to make and own mistakes. They are mentally and physically energetic, independent, able to generate enthusiasm in others for their ideas, and bursting with initiative.

Strategists. They easily move from systems thinking and intellectual discussions to practical solutions and interactions tailored to their various audiences.

"Super STARs"—Separating the Haves from the Have Mores

In 1998, Richard Kelley published his book, *How To Be A STAR At*

Work, listing and explaining nine strategies that would propel workers from average producers to "STAR" producers, thus enhancing their value to themselves and their current employers. Because these star behaviors speak so well to the entrepreneurial and strategic assets of the "Knowledge Nomad," we are including the essence of his work in this chapter. It is important to note that Kelley has incontrovertible evidence that "stars are created, not just born."

Before introducing the behaviors, Kelley provides some principles that must accompany individual performance. Workers must be able to:

- Distinguish between form and substance; or recognize the difference between those people who are promoted to their level of incompetence (the "Peter Principle") and those who have earned their reputations because they embody the entire star performer model;
- Prove their worth to managers, colleagues, *and* customers daily; and
- Incorporate all nine work "breakthrough strategies" together to achieve great results; being good at just one or two won't work.

The Nine Work Strategies that Build Productivity and Innovative Added Value

1. Initiative: Blazing trails in the organization's white spaces.
2. Networking: Knowing who knows by plugging into the knowledge network.
3. Self-Management: Managing your whole life at work.
4. Perspective: Getting the big picture.
5. Followership: Checking your ego at the door to lead in assists.
6. Teamwork: Getting real about teams.
7. Leadership: Doing Small-L leadership in a Big-L world.
8. Organizational Savvy: Using street smarts in the corporate power zone.
9. Show-and-Tell: Persuading your audience with the right message.

Initiative. Going above and beyond the accepted job description, offering value-adding ideas, and doing so for the benefit of coworkers or the entire organization is the first behavior Kelley introduces. Once ideas are proposed, initiative also assumes implementing new ideas; initiative involves creativity and risk.

Networking. Star producers understand networking to be developing reliable pathways to knowledge experts who are able to help bring critical tasks to fruition. Conversely, star producers share their knowledge with those who need it. Their goal is to eradicate the knowledge deficit inherent in every job.

Self-Management. This behavior moves well beyond managing time and projects better; self-management serves to seek and find creative opportunities, direct work choices, ensure high performance, and carve out career paths. Self-management means developing talents and experiences to enhance value to employers.

Perspective. Perspective is the skill that allows workers to grasp the multi-dimensionality of a project or problem within its largest context; it also means that the views and concerns of "critical others"—customers, competitors, coworkers, and bosses—are understood and considered in proposed and implemented solutions. Broad perspectives encourage workers to evaluate the relative importance of myriad viewpoints when considering product or service improvements or solutions.

Followership. Followership is the ability to be actively engaged in helping the organization succeed while practicing independent, constructive, and critical judgment of goals, tasks, and procedures. It means working cooperatively with a leader to accomplish organizational goals despite personality differences or contrary personal views.

Teamwork. Teamwork involves taking joint ownership for all team activities—goal setting, work activities, scheduling, and group accomplishments - both positive and negative. It also involves making positive contributions to a team effort, encouraging others to feel part of the team, dealing with conflict, and supporting others in their team activities.

Leadership. Leadership is a work strategy that uses individual expertise and influence to convince a group to unite around a substantial task. The roles of leadership are diverse and include helping the group establish a clear vision of what they want to accomplish, garnering the resources necessary to ensure the task's completion, instilling the necessary levels of commitment and trust, and shepherding the project to successful completion. It is *not* about positional authority or flaunting titles.

Organizational Savvy. Schmoozing with the right people in the workplace does not constitute organizational savvy. This strategy enables worker to navigate an organization's competing interests, promote cooperation, address conflicts, and produce results. It involves managing successfully individual and group dynamics, knowing when to avoid and when to meet conflicts, and knowing how to make allies of potential "enemies."

Show-and-Tell. Selecting information to pass to others and developing the most effective user-friendly format for reaching and persuading a specific audience are the heart and soul of this behavior. At its most sophisticated level, show-and-tell means selecting the right message for a particular audience or the appropriate audience for a specific message. Although slick presentations may have their place, they are not for the purposes of impressing upper management. This skill does not include the need to be recognized.

In summary, through exhaustive evaluative studies, these strategies have shown dramatic results. Kelly's evaluations showed that women, minorities, and newer workers employing these behaviors received overall improvement ratings 400 percent greater than their coworkers not practicing the nine behaviors. The impact on corporate "bottom lines" was equally dramatic. The long-range fiscal benefits continued to accumulate each year, eclipsing the initial corporate investment within the first year. Most importantly in our view, workers reported higher levels of work satisfaction, professional growth, and collegiality.

Chapter Implications

- Knowledge is the most valued commodity in today's economy; workers who understand this and have adapted accordingly are the ones able to capitalize on the best and most creative employment opportunities.
- Increasingly, workers will be independent contractors or "free agents." As such, they will practice autonomy, have facility with technology, embrace ambiguity, and be highly mobile.
- Those workers wanting to distinguish themselves within and outside of work organizations need to exceed traditional expectations. "STAR" behaviors are becoming the goal, raising the bar for performance and value-added contributions.
- Employers are increasingly less interested in "repairing workers" and are spending more time evaluating the character traits behind the workers in whom they most want to invest.
- "Knowledge Nomads" envelope "STAR" behaviors, see lifelong learning as the fuel for success, agility as their password, and optimism as their mind set as they continually master the trade-offs of globalization and technology.

CHAPTER 6

Education: The Fuel Behind Mastery, Performance and Hope

"Now and then I see an example of classroom learning that braids together the different strands of nontraditional education, a lesson that is collaborative, interdisciplinary, project-based, dedicated to discovery, animated by student decision-making, and grounded in the construction of meaning."

Alfie Kohn *The Schools Our Children Deserve* (1999, p. 156)

Globalization, technology, nomadic workers and employers, accelerated rates of change, increasing competition! Success for life now more than ever hinges on acquiring new basic skills and a commitment to lifelong learning. Yet, how well are our educational systems equipped and supported to impart these talents? What do our educational systems need to "look like"? What should students be learning? How should they be taught to improve performance? When change is needed, how can it be done efficiently and humanely?

This chapter compiles the results of and lessons learned from various school reform efforts. We begin with data on the earnings benefits of education. We next cover recent legislation prompting current school reforms, and end with our conclusions and suggestions for changes. Our hope is that we can provide salient information to foster interest in educational discussions. Progressively, each and every American citizen is a part of school reform, responsible for and accountable to our economic prosperity and individual well being.

While many fault public education, it is important to note that since 1946 the American education system has educated a larger and larger share of the student population. As Carnavale states so eloquently,

It's not that American education failed...it's that other things changed...what changed was the economic environment in which education operated, and the relationships between education and the economy. What changed, essentially, were the demands that are made on American education to fully employ, to provide a family wage, to provide sufficient human capital to maintain American families, to provide a quality of opportunity, and to make the American economy grow (Carnevale, 2004).

Why Education? Emerging Employment Trends?

Education is directly linked to the types and availability of jobs. In the past 40 years, American employment reality has changed from "job certainty" to creating one's own position, escalating the emphasis on education. In 1973, only 28% of workers had any postsecondary education (see Table 6). In 2000, 59% of workers had at least some college. The proportion of workers with an associate degree, certificate, or some college has more than doubled from 12% to 28%. Workers with bachelor's degrees have more than doubled as well, from 9% in 1973 to 20% in 2000; in the same time frame, graduate degree holders increased from 7% to 11%.

Table 6. Changes in Job Distribution in the United States

	1959	1979	2000	Difference 1959-2000
Office Jobs	29.8%	34.9%	38.5%	+8.7
Education and Health-care Jobs	10.2%	14.2%	15.3%	+5.1
Technology Jobs	3.4%	4.9%	7.0%	+3.6
Factory Jobs	31.7%	24.1%	17.2%	-14.5
Low-skilled Services Jobs	20.3%	19.8%	20.6%	+0.3
Farm Jobs	4.6%	2.2%	1.4%	-3.2
	100.0%	100.0%	100.0%	

Note: As reported by Carnevale & Desrochers (2003, p. 229).

When we examine trends from 1973 to 2000 (see Table 7), the change in need for educational attainment is quite apparent. In 1973, one half of factory workers had dropped out of high school. Today, workers with post high school educations fill factory jobs not displaced by technology. The demand for health-care, technology, and education employees has pressed the growth of those with certificates, as well as associate, bachelor, graduate, and professional degrees. Although entry-level, low-skill positions do exist, they no longer offer livable wages.

Table 7. Distribution of Educational Attainment in the Workforce

	1973	2000	Difference 1973-2000
High School Dropout	32.0%	9.5%	-22.5
High School Graduate	40.1%	31.7%	-8.4
Some College	12.1%	28.1%	+16.0%
Associate Degree	—	18.3%	—
No Degree	—	9.8%	—
Bachelor's Degree	8.7%	20.1%	+11.4
Graduate Degree	7.1%	10.7%	+3.6
	100.0%	100.0%	

Note: The data in 1973 do not allow a breakout among associate degree holders and those who received some postsecondary education but no degree. As reported by Carnevale & Desrochers (2003, p. 230).

Tracking the most and least educated workers from 1959 through 1998, shows the clear fiscal value of education. Since 1959, in general, the earnings of those with the greatest education levels rose the most; although men with some college or less have seen declines in their inflation-adjusted earnings (See Table 8). Women at all educational levels show increased earnings.

The most compelling example of education and wages is the comparison of male and female workers with postsecondary education to high school graduates. According to the U.S. Department of Commerce Census Bureau (2002), based on 1999 dollars, the average life-time earnings of workers with different levels of education are as follows

High school graduates	$1.2 million
Bachelor's degrees	$2.1 million
Master's degrees	$2.5 million
Doctoral degrees	$3.4 million
Professional degrees	$4.4 million

(Note: These projections are based on a work life spanning ages 25 through 64).

Table 8. Earnings and Educational Attainment

	1959	1979	1998	%Change 1979-1998
Men				
Total	$29,700	$42,500	$44,600	+4.9%
High School Dropout	$24,100	$30,300	$23,300	-23.1%
High School Graduate	$32,200	$40,100	$33,800	-15.7%
Some College/ Associate Degree	$38,400	$44,300	$41,300	-6.7%
Bachelor's Degree	$48,100	$54,900	$59,800	+8.9%
Graduate Degree	$47,000	$58,800	$76,500	+30.0%
Women				
Total	$12,700	$19,100	$26,600	+39.2%
High School Dropout	$10,200	$13,300	$13,800	+3.8%
High School Graduate	$13,900	$17,400	$20,400	+17.3%
Some College/ Associate Degree	$15,900	$19,800	$25,800	+30.3%
Bachelor's Degree	$19,800	$23,500	$34,700	+47.7%
Graduate Degree	$25,700	$32,300	$46,600	+44.3%

Note: Earnings are for prime-age workers (30 to 59) years old) in 2000 dollars. As reported by Carnevale & Desrochers, 2003, p. 231).

Educational Accountability and Standards-Based Reform: A Bit of History

Since the 1970's, schools have been responding to charges of "...the anonymity and lack of accountability endemic to large, impersonal and bureaucratically organized institutions, the fragmentation of a departmentalized curriculum with little discernible connection to what young people want or imagine they need to know, and the isolation of schools from the community..." (Steinberg & Cohen, 2002, p. 1). Schools, believing that emphasizing and increasing performance standards for students would enhance achievement and allay public criticisms, launched what is familiarly known as standards-based reforms.

Standards-based reform has mixed results. It has led to higher standardized test scores, but primarily for those students who already identify with academic achievement goals, and chiefly in those schools with the fiscal capacity for instructional improvements. In some cases, standards-based school reform has resulted in more challenging and relevant curricula. Unfortunately, however, setting higher standards has not alleviated the crisis of growing student alienation and dropout rates common in urban high schools (Steinberg & Cohen, 2002).

What it has done is illuminate the "economic segregation" plaguing our nation's schools, raising serious questions about the adequacy of local property tax funding without federal and state supplements. Although some states are attempting system redesigns that include (a) defining the resources needed for students in low income areas to reach state standards, (b) funneling funds to low-income schools to offset inadequate local taxes, and (c) encouraging Washington to help equalize the startling discrepancies (Symonds, 2002) their efforts are futile more often than not given the current federal and state deficits.

Standards-based school reform has garnered its fair share of critics. Holding schools accountable for test scores and subsequently determining funding on the basis of their outcomes, contradicts the data about how students learn and what tests can and cannot measure. As stated by Meier (2002),

> That a standardized one-size-fits-all test could be invented and imposed by the state, that teachers could unashamedly teach to such a test, that all students could theoretically succeed at this test, and that it could be true to any form of serious intellectual or technical psychometric standards is just plain impossible. (p. 192)

After compiling evidence from considerable research, Kohn (1999) published what he terms the "Five Fatal Flaws" of the tougher standards movement. Our interpretation of his work follows:

- A *disproportionate focus on achievement*—Primarily focusing on results is simplistic and detrimental to learning. Students should be thinking about improving their performance; the preoccupation with achievement is very different from the focus on learning.
- *Learning as memorizing* discrete facts—Although modern cognitive science explains why rote, disparate facts are not conducive to learning, the tougher standards movement continues to treat learners as inert objects. Basic skills and core knowledge

are bits of information expected to be retold by students in non-meaningful ways.

- *Standardized tests as true measures of student achievement*—Increased educational excellence and higher standards are typically measured by higher test scores and that is what schools are pressed to produce. This is a short-sighted view of education; indeed, teaching to the test rarely promotes real learning.
- *Forcing educational improvement* by specifying exactly what must be taught and learned—Mandating a particular kind of education is not an effective way to compel teachers and students to change and do things differently. Such methods fly in the face of all we know about successful educational change.
- *Harder is better*—Harder is not necessarily better; in fact it is a negligent oversimplification of teaching and learning. Essentially, judging textbooks, teachers, and students by "harder" standards is perpetuating the assumption that if something isn't working well, then insist on more of the same and that will solve the problem.

No Child Left Behind: Another Educational Reform Intervention

In 2001, when the legislature renewed the *Elementary and Secondary Education Act No Child Left Behind* (NCLB), they believed they were addressing general concerns of overall satisfactory student achievement and the particular "achievement gap" between minority and majority students. The NCLB Act has galvanized state efforts to raise academic standards, measure results, and hold schools and students accountable for improving achievement. Carnavale calls it, "…truly the most interventionist and aggressive federal action in American education, especially with respect to the intervention of federal law into state and local educational policies since desegregation" (Carnevale, 2004). For some states, the Act is pushing farther and faster reforms; for others, it presents unparalleled challenges for setting and maintaining the direction of school reform. Regardless, all states face critical, often competing issues to their long-term reform labors as they implement the Act's requirements.

Key Provisions of NCLB Legislation
Although the actual legislation is 1,400 hundred pages, there are only a few critical components. Every state is charged with instituting the following NCLB key provisions:
- Challenging, coherent content standards in reading and math set immediately, with science standards by 2005-06;
- Grade-by-grade reading and math tests in grades 3 through 8 by

2005-06, with science tests in elementary, middle and high school by 2007-08;
- Detailed reporting to schools and the public using results disaggregated by race, ethnicity, economic status, migrant status, English proficiency, gender, and disability by 2002-03;
- Targets for "Adequate Yearly Progress" (AYP) based on 2001-02 test results set by January 2003;
- Assistance to schools missing AYP for two consecutive years in 2004-05;
- Corrective action in schools missing AYP for four consecutive years in 2006-07;
- All schools must employ "highly qualified teachers";
- Counseling-related programs such as school-wide improvement, elementary and secondary school counseling, dropout prevention, transition services, and parental involvement opportunities; and
- Ten percent of all *Title I* funds must be spent on professional development.

NCLB and Changing Leadership Roles

Although fairly prescriptive with its expectations and mandates, NCLB has left many of the most important decisions to state policymakers who traditionally have been driving standards-based reform. States are taking this opportunity to align standards and tests, develop relevant outcome proficiencies, incorporate measurement results into decision making, and provide support for low-performing schools.

NCLB legislation has placed greater and different demands on local education leaders. The act reflects and reinforces a major shift in thinking about the roles and responsibilities of school board members, district superintendents, and principals. Adjusting to NCLB requirements, school and district *leaders face substantial challenges* such as
- Assisting staff in dealing with tougher accountability measures and increasing public scrutiny;
- Understanding assessment instruments and systems, particularly as they relate to identifying performance gaps;
- Selecting curricula that are robust and comprehensive, teach what the tests measure, yet aren't just "drill and practice" test-preparations;
- Establishing meaningful, relevant, data-driven decision making to undergird all educational decisions (Anthes, 2002; Daggett, 2003a);
- Balancing the need to illustrate academic achievement on specific standardized tests with the need to provide overall, less measurable development of students.

The NCLB has not been around long enough to truly measure its effects on education and its needed reforms. Agreeing that no child should be left behind is simple—it reflects the most basic of American ideology. However, getting consensus that all students do not start with the same set of skills, learn at the same level or in the same way, or learn in the same amount of time remains a complex issue. It deserves ongoing debate and timely resolution. As *America's Children: Key Indicators of Well-Being* (Interagency Forum on Child and Family Statistics, 2002) illustrated, America's youth face many challenges as they negotiate school, work, and the larger community. Thoughtful, timely, and meaningful planning to help students navigate a school system continually facing reform with aspirations to match their strengths and interests has never been more important.

What Have We Learned?

First of all, where have we gone wrong? Why have so many of our well-intended actions proven misguided? Cuban (1993) suggests seven phases of reform that challenge communities to agree on why, how, and what students should learn:

1. Social, political, and economic changes in conditions of life or in ideologies create solutions that opinion makers in society define as problems.
2. Policy makers, academics, and opinion makers, such as journalists and top corporate officials (outsiders to the educational enterprise) [develop consensus] about what the problems are and what solutions are feasible.
3. Groups and individuals outside the schools develop policy proposals and programs to solve the perceived problem.
4. Through various mechanisms (legislation, pilot projects, school board decisions) groups and individuals connected to the educational enterprise come to be known as reformers, and press insiders to adopt and implement reforms.
5. As policies get adopted, superintendents, principals, and teachers are disjointed in their efforts to implement these policies.
6. Growing criticism of educators' seemingly slow or halfhearted efforts to implement reforms draw attention away from whether or not schools are solving the problems defined earlier in the reform process. Disappointment sets in.
7. Social, economic, or demographic conditions in society again shift and the cycle begins anew (p.244).

Too Much, Too Quickly
Consensus seems to indicate that generally we didn't heed successful

change practices. Too often, change was mandated—those most keenly affected (i.e., teachers and students) were seldom involved in making the decisions. Leadership support was usually inadequate; in fact, leaders themselves were frequently not clear about the mandated changes, much less informed about how to support large systemic changes. When leadership support was available, it was either only at the beginning of the process or removed too early to have any lasting benefit. Chaos, confusion, disappointment, and resistance were seen as obstacles to be avoided, rather than recognized as natural reactions to change and excellent opportunities for growth. For the most part, the "human emotional" elements of change were ignored.

Leaders, teachers, students, and parents were asked to do too much. That is to say, they remained accountable for the "regular" teaching-learning retinue *and* were expected to modify curricula, rearrange class schedules, attend multiple meetings, develop new teaching plans, and encourage more input from various constituents. Class sizes were large, discipline remained challenging, and support from administration attenuated over time. Additionally, teachers, students, and parents were generally provided only with information about the need to adopt new educational practices; they were seldom given an opportunity to understand or experience their benefits. Essentially, we tried to do too much, too quickly with too few resources, too little support, and too little understanding of what change entails.

Faulty Assumptions

As microcosms of our larger society, schools reflect societal beliefs and norms. As is true across all of society, success is alleged to be determined by one's genes, inborn intelligence, and will (Comer, 2002). Schools have thus given rise to the same social strata that reinforce our definitions of success and thus marginalize so many U.S. citizens. To impede the spread of such marginalization, Dr. Comer (2002) suggests that schools reexamine their founding principles and initiate and emphasize three crucial developmental activities. He proposes that schools:

- Address the problems of marginalized children, families, and communities across society by creating schools that focus on physical health, mental health, and child development in the context of academic learning. They should provide opportunities for constructive self-expression and teach effective interaction skills to help connect marginalized children to the mainstream.
- Change their structures and processes that create the negative social constructs by incorporating child development theory in all practices and providing extensive support services. Leadership and learning academics should focus on helping educators learn to help children develop, rather than simply teach how to impart

knowledge.
- Change cultural beliefs by denouncing those structures that make it acceptable for poor or isolated African-American, Hispanic, or Caucasian students to underachieve. Create school cultures where they are expected to do well and where *all children must gain a good education*.

Another researcher, Steinberg (1996) lends support to the preceding suppositions with findings about the factors outside of school that negatively influence school achievement. After significant study, he concluded that:

> No curricular overhaul, no instructional innovation, no change in school organization, no toughening of standards...will succeed if students do not come to school interested in, and committed to, learning...how we can reengage students in the business of learning, we need to look, not at what goes on inside the classroom, but at students' lives outside the schools' walls. Until we do just this, school reform will fail to improve. (p. 19)

Educational Reform: Everyone's Responsibility
Solving America's achievement problem cannot be done only by schools — schools, parents, employers, the mass media, politicians, and ultimately students need to be involved. In 1996, Laurence Steinberg made ten recommendations for addressing appropriate school reform. We find them relevant today as points of departure for discussions.
1. Refocus the discussion — reform will not work unless we recognize the problem as considerably more far-reaching and complicated than simply changing curricular strands or teaching methods.
2. Establish academic excellence as a national priority — schooling is the primary activity of childhood and adolescence; doing well in school is more important than socializing, sports, or working after school.
3. Increase parental effectiveness — the high rate of parental irresponsibility has reached epidemic proportions; we must address it.
4. Increase parental involvement in school — schools must expand efforts to actively draw parents into school programs.
5. Make school performance really count — scholastic records need to matter more to universities and employers; not having them count marginalizes student achievement efforts.
6. Adopt a system of national standards and examinations — adopt a system of minimum national standards and performance-based

examination for promotions and graduation within American schools.

7. Develop uniform national standards for school transcripts — currently, we have no way of communicating readily-understood information about a student's academic accomplishments to parents, employers, or educators.

8. Eliminate remedial education at four-year colleges and universities — it trivializes the significance of the high school diploma, diminishes the meaning of college admission, erodes the value of college degrees, and drains precious resources away from college-level instruction.

9. Support appropriate school-sponsored extracurricular activities — participation in school-sponsored extracurricular activities strengthens student commitment to school and carries benefits that spill over into the classroom.

10. Limit time for after-school jobs — heavy work commitments significantly interfere with school achievement and scholastic commitment; it is also linked to higher rates of teenage drug and alcohol use.

What Appears to Work?

In this section, we present findings from educators who have dedicated significant portions of their professional lives to the betterment of educational practices. Although their suggestions are diverse, they also contain several commonalities. Perhaps these commonalities are expressed most poignantly by Kohn (1999):

> In place of superficial facts, we emphasize deep understanding. In place of fragmentation, we seek to integrate; we bring together skills, topics and disciplines in a meaningful context. In place of student passivity and isolation, we value learning that is both active and interactive. If there is a unifying theme in all these prescriptions and a common characteristic of the best classrooms, it is that kids are taken seriously (p. 131).

In a recent web cast on "High Schools That Work," Bottoms (2003) suggested that those high schools that:

- Establish a culture of higher expectations in both academic and career-technical classrooms have a greater percentage of students who meet academic performance goals and are better prepared for employment and further study.
- Commit to teaching career-oriented students a solid academic

core and provide extra help to meet the standards produce significantly higher student achievement.

- Focus student efforts on the relationship between classroom work and postsecondary work motivate student achievement in both academic and career and technical studies.

Spawned by lessons learned from *Breaking Ranks: Changing an American Institution* (1996), the sequel, *Breaking Ranks II: Strategies for Leading High School Reform* (National Association of Secondary School Principals, 2004), cites "seven cornerstone strategies" for improving student performance:

1. *Core Knowledge*: Establish the essential learning students need to graduate and adjust curriculum and teaching strategies so they realize graduation.
2. *Connections with Students*: Increase the quantity and improve the quality of student, teacher, and other school personnel interactions by reducing the number of students for which any one adult is responsible.
3. *Personalized Planning*: Implement a comprehensive advisory program ensuring each student plans and assesses his/her academic and social progress.
4. *Adapting to Differences*: Ensure teachers use various instructional strategies and assessments to meet individual learning styles.
5. *Flexible Use of Time*: Allow flexible scheduling for teacher teaming and lesson planning.
6. *Distributed Leadership*: Allow students, teachers, family, and community members, meaningful involvement in decision making.
7. *Continuous Professional Development*: Align staff professional development with content knowledge and instructional strategies students need for graduation.

In his newly released study *America's Most Successful High Schools—What Makes Them Work,* Daggett (2004b) cites the following findings from schools with proven high levels of student success:

- Small learning communities that focus instruction around student interests, learning styles, and aptitudes;
- Curriculum and instruction that emphasizes not only the development of skills, but also their application with business and postsecondary partnerships; and
- A commonly held philosophy that high academic standards are essential for *all students* to ensure their success in the workplace (as jobs for the unskilled are disappearing in the U.S.).

In *Jobs and the Skills Gap* (Daggett, 2003b) addresses the business community's concern about entry-level workers with inadequate reading proficiency. To counteract this deficiency, educators are encouraged to rethink reading competency. Literacy has changed—it is no longer a matter of simply being able to read literature. While certainly culturally important, traditional reading does not address the work place need of proficient "informational reading." Literacy needs to be redefined so that reading and understanding documents and quantitative materials is as important as reading prose, poetry, and other forms of literature. Moreover, reading needs to be part of all content areas not segregated to English language arts.

Crisis or Possibility? Conversations About the American High School (Lewis, 2004) summarizes discussions among state governors, chief state school officers, the U.S. Office of Vocational and Adult Education, the National High School Alliance, and other reform groups on transforming the general-purpose high school into a high-quality learning organization for the 21st century. These groups agreed on the following themes:

1. Aligning educational systems from kindergarten through college (K-16);
2. College preparation as the default high school curriculum;
3. Greater teacher competence, both in content and in pedagogy (some teachers receive no child development training; others as little as one course; teachers must be prepared to work across disciplines in smaller learning communities);
4. Interventions in the early grades to ensure that students can read at grade level by the time they reach high school;
5. Attention to the high dropout rate so that more than a few students finish college; and
6. Greater use of small-scale learning environments in high schools.

Educational Environments: Education Is Not Just About Subject Matter

It appears students can adhere to common standards, but through different pedagogies, different institutional arrangements, and in significantly different amounts of time. Experimental programs creating smaller high schools (the "smaller is better" movement) are proving to promote higher student achievement levels and higher graduation and lower dropout rates; and they are safer than larger schools. Moreover, small schools appear to make the most difference for low-income and minority youth. A codification blending of youth development approaches with contextual and authentic learning (see Table 9) within smaller schools has demonstrated remarkable success in high school and postsecondary graduation rates (Steinberg & Allen, 2002).

Table 9. The Five C's

Caring	Caring relationships that help young people build an attachment to the learning environment and provide them with the support they need to overcome obstacles
Cognitive	Cognitive challenges that engage young people intellectually and help them develop the competencies they will need for postsecondary success
Culture	Culture of support for effort that pushes young people to do their best work
Community	Community, contribution, voice, and leadership in a group that young people feel is worth belonging to
Connections	Connections to high-quality postsecondary learning and career opportunities through an expanding network of adults

The U.S. is a democratic society, yet we do little to help our citizens understand their civic responsibilities. Schools that foster social responsibility, sometimes referred to as "social capital," create conditions to stimulate students to use their strengths in socially relevant ways. Although this notion is frequently surrounded by political controversy, schools that do embrace this character development component claim their students demonstrate "... the values, norms, networks, and social trust ... geared toward the greater public good" (Renzulli, 2002, p. 34).

Schools themselves can create climates of mutual respect, dignity, safety, and nurturance that have proven to promote student achievement, particularly that of students considered "at-risk." What might these climates entail? We were so taken by the sentiments expressed in a recent article by a guidance counselor (Silva, 2004) describing her southwestern school we are including our interpretation of her points. Recounting her school as one whose overall goal is to help its students confront the profound questions of life, she notes that administrators and teachers have defined core values that guide their actions. Their creed might look like this:

- We ask students to develop their minds meaningfully and creatively.
- We believe in fairness—all goals apply to all students equally.
- We believe in personalizing teaching and learning.
- We pursue with passion the dual goals of student-as-learner/worker and teacher-as-coach.

- We assess students on their performance of real, relevant, meaningful tasks.
- We perpetuate through practice the principles of decency.
- We reflect the values of a democratic community in all we do.

Transforming Education—What Should Our Classrooms Look Like?

Although typically more responsive to change than leading it, educational systems are integrating more and more of the new worker components. Schools are working toward contextual learning—consider team teaching, applied learning strategies, overarching capstone experiences—however, there is still much they could incorporate. In Table 10 we've compiled the thoughts of some of education's foremost thinkers on how our learning environments might be evaluated. Listed as demonstrable learner skills and teacher traits, they support the acquisition of those characteristics needed by workers in the transformed workplaces.

Table 10. Learner Skills and Teacher Attributes for the Transformed Workplace

Learner Skills

- Abstract systems thinking and problem solving
- Experimentation process
- Team building and team membership
- Comfort with ambiguity
- Passion for lifelong learning
- Creativity
- Entrepreneurship
- Process thinking (understanding the big picture)
- Familiarity with chaos theory
- Agility
- Technological fluency and literacy
- Communications (including public-speaking and presentation-design skills
- Leadership and followership
- Seeking, valuing and incorporating cultural diversity in choices
- Knowledge of cultural anthropology
- Mastery of the tenets of democratic societies
- One or two foreign languages, including Portuguese, Spanish, Japanese, Mandarin, Korean, Malay

Table 10 cont.

Teacher Attributes

- Experts in their disciplines (e.g., math, science)
- Hold high expectations for their students
- Insist on innovation and creativity from their students
- Maintain curriculum focus on "life-long" and "long-life" skills

---

Adapted from Daggett (2003c); Feller (2003); Hinds (2003) & Thornburg (2002).

Schools must insist on learning as lifelong. Events that influence all our major life decisions occur too often and too rapidly for us to believe that once we graduate we've learned all we need to know. Employers are faced with burgeoning competition almost momentarily. Long-range planning can be reduced to a few weeks. Additionally, the U.S. Department of Labor, Bureau of Labor Statistics (2004) reports that workers hold 10.2 jobs between the ages of 18 and 38. These jobs were defined as, "...an unintended period of work with a particular employee." Although job change decreases with age, learning to learn quickly within new contexts is still important. Not knowing how to learn independently or minimizing its importance to employment success can prove fatal to a meaningful career.

School Reform and Career Development

Consider the following recent findings (Daggett, 2003c).
- The U.S. spends the most per capita on education of all nations surveyed. Yet, the overall literacy rate barely matches the world average.
- U.S. Literacy rates are lower for young adults compared to young adults of other nations.
- Changing demographics worsen the U.S. literacy problem. The fastest growing segments of the U.S. population (minorities) and the youngest adults (ages 16-36) are the least literate in comparison to other developed nations. To a significant extent, these groups will comprise the future work force.
- As well-paying, low-skilled jobs continue to be replaced by technology, a growing segment of the population with low literacy (including technical literacy) levels is becoming functionally unemployable.
- The U.S. spends far above the international average on higher education (for the more literate) and well below the international average for basic adult education (for the least literate).

At a time when the U.S. clearly needs to rethink its educational priorities and what most students suggest is "irrelevancy," we have the confounding philosophy prompted by *No Child Left Behind*. Most likely unintentionally, the legislation fosters the notion that the core academic courses in math, science, and English language arts need more curricular emphasis at the expense of career and technical education, the arts, and foreign languages. "*...The opposite is actually true*" (Daggett, 2003a, p. 3).

Daggett (2003a) notes that specialized programs (i.e., career development), when enriched by curricular modifications that deliver academics, play to students' interests, learning styles, and aptitudes. These types of programs have appeal to many students, especially those most difficult to serve and those within the nine subgroups monitored by AYP. To prevent marginalization within and potential elimination from school curricula, career development programs must demonstrate clearly that they:

- Are contributing to the academic success of students;
- Serve as motivation for students to remain in school and perform at higher levels in academic classes; and
- Encourage students to pursue education beyond high school graduation.

In short, career management programs must be able to prove that they both meet the workplace competency demands *and* contribute significantly to students gaining academic proficiencies as measured by state assessments/ tests (Daggett, 2004a; Daggett, 2003c).

Reflections

As Posner (2002) stated, "It is a tricky business trying to guess what experiences will motivate an individual to intellectual achievement or what skills or bits of knowledge will wind up being important in a person's life" (p. 316). However, as the primary shapers and facilitators of student career development within schools, school counselors owe students their best thinking. For their parts, students need to maximize their strengths, be more self-directed, and demonstrate the self-discipline needed to get what they want in life and work. They need encouragement during all experiences so they can learn to evaluate options, critically evaluate decision outcomes, and assume responsibility for garnering the career development competencies they need. At the very least, school counselors need to help students learn to ask better questions such as those listed below and work with more realistic assumptions that reflect an understanding of the changing workplace.

- What motivates you...what gets the best from you?
- What are you curious about? (entrepreneurial thoughts)
- How do you plan to get the people skills you need?
- How are you going to get the verbal and presentation skills you need to persuade others or change another's attitude?
- How can we get you to embrace technology? (productivity tools)
- What are the most challenging courses and "stretch assignments" you can stand without saying "uncle"?
- What strengths do you want to focus on?
- How are you becoming more agile, intuitive, and innovative?
- How can you keep your excitement for learning and development alive throughout your career?
- For students moving on to college, rather than just ask, "What do you want to major in?" ask, "What experiences do you want in college?" and "What problems do you want to try to solve as you are sharpening your advanced basic skills?"

It seems certain that students need to be educated for globalization, the "economic, political and cultural force that dominates the developed and developing worlds" (Nordgren, 2002, p. 318). School counselors cognizant of how the workplace is changing can better assist students see how globalization and technology create opportunities. This can best be done by instilling in students:

- Creativity and other entrepreneurial skills;
- Attitudes that generate excitement and energy toward new career opportunities;
- Intra and interpersonal communication and team building skills;
- Independent thinking, problem-solving skills, and persuasion skills;
- The imagination and agility to adapt to change as the norm;
- The character traits and strength to develop and act from a principled, ethical core; and
- Faith and trust in one's abilities to negotiate life's challenges.

In addition to promoting these key elements and persuasively arguing for curriculum change, excellence and equity, and rigor and relevancy, school counselors and career development specials need to focus on preparing students for a lifetime of learning and work transitions - a lifetime in which one's goals and resources need to be complementary if students are to acquire a sense of mastery and hope.

Much as school counselors and career specialists do for youth, career development professionals need to play the role of advocate, broker, and coach for adults and employees. Through development planning and "gap analysis," career specialists offer adults access to education that can pay dividends in present jobs while building assets for the next transition. In the age of the knowledge worker, education is the fuel behind mastery, performance, and hope.

Chapter Implications

- Educational attainment is increasingly and more critically important to career and life success. A *passion* for lifelong learning is as important as one's commitment to learning.
- While educational achievement can affect economic opportunities, it is no more important than learning the skills needed to be an active, conscientious citizen.
- School reform is complex—questioning our fundamental assumptions and involving all constituents (i.e., educational leaders, businesses, community members, political leaders, parents, teachers, and students) in decision-making are crucial to its success.
- School reform is also about societal changes—without addressing parental involvement, economic disparities, cultural differences and values, student activities outside of school, and socialization issues school reform will fall short.
- Meaningful, relevant, exciting content is not the only key to student achievement. School environments are critical elements to student success, particularly to those students with high support needs.
- Schooling in the 21st century is dramatically different from that of previous centuries. Knowledge is defined differently; and whereas character development was once considered a parental responsibility, it is now difficult to separate it from content curriculum.
- Continuous learning and development plans that help adults and employees address a "gap analysis" are essential for improving job performance and personal development.

CHAPTER 7

Challenging Career Development Assumptions

"Changes in work and the workplace require a concomitant revision of career theory and practice. ...Career development specialists focus on the nexus between person and environment, that is, the psycho-social integration of individuals into society. As such, career services benefit society as well as individuals."

(Savickas, 2000, p. 61) *Making Waves: Career Development and Public Policy*

Developing comprehensive career plans is critical for all individuals as they navigate the white waters of change and transitions. Adults will need higher levels of career management as they experience greater amounts of workplace change. Many will be displaced by technology; others will see their jobs outsourced. Employed adults will need managerial support as they close learning gaps, prevent career derailment, or resolve conflicts - particularly when profit margins decrease. Organizations, struggling to find and keep talent essential to their competitive advantage in a global marketplace, will rely more on in-house career development systems.

Schools are working diligently to implement the *No Child Left Behind* (NCLB) legislation, often at the expense of career development interventions and programs. Regardless of the populations that career development professionals serve, many of the assumptions underlying their efforts and tools are no longer relevant in the Diamond Shaped emerging workplace described in Chapter 4.

In this chapter, we focus on shifting career development assumptions and their implications for career development professionals. We propose new career development assumptions and offer suggestions to career development professionals about the skills they might consider using to incorporate the new assumptions. (For information on teaching career counselors, see Feller & Davies, 1999; and for new assessment tools useful with adults, see Feller, 2003). Our ultimate goal is to provide resources and insights to career development professionals who can help students and clients create more meaningful career and life plans.

Career Development Assumptions: Keeping Pace with the Times

Changing workplace needs and employer demands require different worker readiness skills; consequently, assumptions about careers and their attendant development need overhauling. As with every major shift, we must tailor our skills to suit the times. Shifting assumptions impact how career development professionals do their jobs. Table 11 compares a set of traditional assumptions to what we see as emerging career development assumptions.

We argue that challenging old assumptions can lead practitioners to reframe how they see and conduct their work. Such efforts can lead to more progressive ways of fostering student development. The list of emerging assumptions encapsulates:

- What we know about pedagogy from the science of cognition;
- The importance of education promoting "social capital" and character development through what some have called "apprenticeships in democracy";
- The emergent worker skills for competing successfully in the changing workplace;
- The need for hope when deciding career goals;
- The value of beginning career development activities early in the educational experience;
- The redefinition of school-to-work as a process rather than an event;
- A new vision for school counseling programs; and
- A new way to re-direct adult careers in transition.

Those advocating career preparation at the expense of student preparation for life roles and as social capital are urged to consider the emerging roles of every citizen and the need for sustainable and peaceful communities. Those convinced that the market-driven global economy enhanced by technology and entrepreneurship is the only way to prosperity, democracy, and security are encouraged to consider the vision of a civil society; or a society committed to "...the values of community, faith, responsibility, civic virtue, neighborliness, stewardship, and mutual concern for each other..."(Yankelovich, 1999, p. 202). Further, communities need to help students develop the character needed to resist ploys leading to corporate scandals and political corruption that quickly undermine institutional trust regardless of how the workplace changes. Career plans of students need to include not only academic and technical skills, but also

Table 11. Comparison of the Traditional to Emerging Career Development Assumptions

Dimension	Traditional Assumptions	Emerging Assumptions
Pedagogy	Students commit bits of knowledge to memory in isolation from practical application; academics are important in and of themselves.	Effective teaching/learning learning motivates students to connect knowledge content with the context of application, developing and utilizing the "thinking brain"; problem-solving and decision-making skills are promoted.
Values	What one values is not as important as ensuring a secure job with vertical mobility.	Identifying values in career planning is critical; giving students the ability to set valued goals, identify strategies to achieve goals, and the motivation to actualize goals is fundamental to career success.
Career Exploration Timeframe	Either the senior year in high school or first year of college is soon enough to begin career discussions.	Career development begins in elementary school and continues through high school and beyond; activities are developmentally appropriate.
Job Longevity	Change is inevitable, BUT secure jobs do exist; find companies where this has proven true and stick with them; rewards will follow.	Security comes from the ability to anticipate, make and manage changes; change is the only constant.
Educational Contexts	School designs and instructional delivery do not matter; "teach to the middle" and all students will progress. Seat time is the constant and learning is the variable.	Not all students learn in the same way, in the same timeframe, or with the same kinds of physical and emotional structures. Honor differences so that learning becomes the constant and time is the variable.
Career Preparation Components	Primary focus is on academic subjects and technical skills; students learn workplace behaviors from parents and/or community members and integration of academic and technical is not needed.	Character development—moral, ethical, affective growth—is equally important to technical skills and academic achievements; schools are responsible for "apprenticeships in democracy."

Table 11 cont.

Meaningful Employment	Students should focus on growth sectors and choose one; know what they want and where they are going, and not to deviate from a plan.	Increased emphasis on spirituality and community in the workplace; the career of choice must have personal meaning; students should have ideas of what they want, and be open to new information.
Job Skills Acquisition	Learn while in school, then one's career is assured; postsecondary degrees are fundamental to success.	Learning is lifelong and everywhere; acquire as much from informal as formal learning; explore needed education. More than half of all jobs require short to moderate training.
Accessing Career Information	Learn about careers independently; the key to success is for students to learn to write their own ticket; they need to make it on their own.	Access allies and become an ally; people progress as much by whom they know, and who knows them, as on what they know.
School Counselor Role	Keep the focus on what school counselors do.	Focus on how students are different because of the school counseling programs and the work of the school counselor.
School to Work Transitions	School-to-work transition is the bridge that connects schools to employers.	School-to-work transition is strengthened through basic skill acquisition and career development outcomes in elementary and middle school, and follows non-linear events which connect school to employment and workplace induction.
Evaluation of School Counseling Programs	Use graduation and college acceptance rates, and amount of financial aid awarded as success metrics.	Attention to success in completing college semesters, amount of debt accrued, satisfaction with high school transition, level of voter participation, commitment to creating social capital.
Re-inventing Careers	Know yourself first, know what you want to do before you act.	Knowing yourself comes as a result of experimenting and testing out new options, and networking and getting feedback from new people

lessons in democracy (Goodlad, 2002), activities to promote developmental assets (Search Institute, 1997), and opportunities to learn to be self-reliant career managers (National Life/Work Centre, n.d.). Taking a global view of career development and the emerging assumptions to be challenged is essential. As school counselors help students plan, it is helpful to note that social advocacy, "...is the heritage of the profession" (Gysbers, 2001, p.103). School counselors overtly and unconsciously impact student options as a result of the assumptions they hold. As a result, the importance of career specialists and school counselors on the longer term development of youth cannot be understated.

Hermina Ibarra, in *Working Identity: Unconventional Strategies for Reinventing Your Career* (2003), offers insightful and creative ways to help adults feeling unfulfilled or burned out, or confronting the realization that they are unhappy with their present life chapter. Unlike many models suggesting that clients must first know what they want to do before they act, Ibarra argues that knowing can only come from doing and experimenting. She lists nine "unconventional strategies" for making a career change. While some are not new, they offer excitement and hope for adults who are stuck in old assumptions about how to explore and grow. They are:

1. Act your way into a new way of thinking and *being*. Start by changing what you are *doing* since you cannot discover yourself through introspection.
2. Stop trying to find your one true self. Focus your attention on which of your *many possible selves* you want to test and learn more about.
3. Allow yourself a transition period in which it is okay to oscillate between holding on and letting go.
4. Resist the temptation to start by making a big decision that will change everything in one fell swoop. Seek small wins and incremental gains.
5. Identify projects that help you explore a new line of work or style of working.
6. Don't just focus on the work. Find people who are what you want to be and get their support through the transition.
7. Don't wait for a cataclysmic moment when the truth is revealed. Find meaning in everyday events.
8. Step back when you are short on insight. Engage in the real world to make discoveries.
9. Seize new opportunities. Change happens in bursts and starts.

Changing Skills for Career Development Professionals

In light of workplace change, emerging career assumptions, the need for employees to continually develop their talents, and school reform efforts, career development professionals face a constant need to acquire new skills and strategies. Currently, facilitating comprehensive career development planning means that professionals need to:

- Understand and clarify their changing roles to focus on enhancing a client or organization's competency attainment;
- Gain knowledge about the needs and idiosyncrasies of various client groups and industries; and
- Remain abreast of workplace change and expanding learning options for clients.

Career Development Professionals: Developing Requisite Talents

Learning about the value of *diversity* (Myers & McCaulley, 1985; Miscisin, 2001); *strength* themes (Buckingham & Clifton, 2001); career *success* strategies (Derr, 1986); *courage* to examine traditional career assumptions (Hansen, 1997; Grey & Herr, 2000; Barry, 2001; Feller, 2003); and the willingness to *question* counseling conventions (Amundson, 2003) are all integral skills for career specialists to master. Facilitating career development plans demands that counselors explore *their* worldviews and continually expose themselves to experiences, models, and techniques that broaden their understanding and empathy. Accumulating varied experiences and practicing humility enhances counselor wisdom and openness to the ways others choose to live their lives (Dominquez & Robin, 1992; Whitmyer, 1994). By cultivating broader perspectives, counselors become effective at instilling hope (Snyder, Feldman, Shorey & Rand, 2002) and belief in self in even the hardest client cases (e.g., "career stallers," Lombardo & Eichinger, 2002a).

As mental health practitioners have come to understand, there is seldom a dichotomy between personal and career counseling. Career development professionals know that career counseling is riddled with emotional and psychological dimensions; work and mental health are tightly interwoven. Consequently, all career development training should include human development and emotional and psychological processes (Herr, 1999; Niles and Pate, 1989).

Tools for Acquiring Counseling Skills

Career development professionals need a practical organizing tool that can help them acquire the skills necessary for their burgeoning roles. One such tool is offered by Hansen's (1997) *Integrative Life Planning* (ILP) approach. Combining accepted theories and proven practices about how people (a) choose jobs or educational pursuits, (b) transition through life stages and cycles, and (c) negotiate psychological and environmental barriers that can immobilize them during career changes, Hansen (1997) gives a comprehensive, interdisciplinary, and eminently practical template for working with clients. Subsuming fundamental and broad life-choice questions, ILP concentrates on *six key life tasks*:

1. Finding work that needs doing in changing global contexts;
2. Weaving lives into a meaningful whole;
3. Connecting family and work;
4. Valuing pluralism and inclusivity;
5. Exploring spirituality and life purpose and
6. Managing personal transitions and organizational change.

Continuing, Hansen (1997) poses seven provocative questions to guide career development professionals in *strategizing individual or organizational change*.

1. How do we help people move from the old to new paradigm, see the big picture, understand the connection between local and global needs and the changes that the twenty-first century is likely to bring?
2. How can individuals achieve greater wholeness when our educational and occupational institutions are still structured on the old Newtonian paradigm, when actual work structures do not keep up with human needs, and when the traditional work ethic, especially in upper management of corporations and institutions, still dominates?
3. How can career professionals help their clients understand the importance of both women's and men's lives and the need for self-sufficiency and connectedness for both? How can both men and women become self-directed agents in their life plans?
4. How can individuals and organizations be helped to understand the link between work and family and to work toward change that will facilitate their connection rather than erect barriers between them?
5. How can career development professionals best help clients negotiate in a different world? How can they help them understand their own uniqueness while valuing the differences of "those others" in the workplace and in other areas of their lives?
6. How can clients be helped to become agents for change themselves?
7. How can career professionals help clients learn to negotiate the various parts of their lives, set priorities, and put the pieces of their own quilts together in meaningful ways? (p. 263).

Unique in both its comprehensiveness and incisiveness, the ILP requires career development professionals to carefully scrutinize all pivotal life choices impacting career development. We would benefit immeasurably in our personal and professional growth by challenging ourselves to ask and answer these questions.

Career Development in the Workplace

Organizations use career development as a means of attracting and keeping talented people (Pink, 2001). They invest in employee development, finding it effective in spurring performance, maintaining bench strength, capturing intellectual capital, fostering innovation, and defining or enhancing organizational identity (Stewart, T., 2001).

When career development interventions such as employee development plans are used by employers, evidence indicates overall improved employee performance, a more engaged workforce, and more effective management. As Michaels, Handfield-Jones, and Axelrod explain in *The War for Talent* (2001), career planning and management is becoming an important weapon in an employer's retention efforts, as well as a strategy for heightened competitiveness.

In *Promoting a Development Culture in Your Organization: Using Career Development as a Change Agent,* Simonsen (1997) offers a comprehensive roadmap for creating a development culture in organizations.

- Employee development plans must be linked to and driven by business needs.
- The organization needs to create and promote a vision and philosophy of career development.
- Senior management must actively and publicly support all efforts.
- Clear communication and comprehensive education for all employees across all organizational levels needs to precede and accompany the plan's implementation.
- Management involvement in learning and mastering all phases of the plan is essential.
- Employees must be given incentives and taught how to assume ownership of and responsibility for their own growth.
- Adequate and appropriate career development resources must be available to all employees.

Maximizing individual employee contribution in organizational outcomes is a matter of eight steps according to *Follow This Path: How the World's Greatest Organizations Drive Growth by Utilizing Human Potential* (Clifton & Gonzalez-Molina, 2002).

1. *Identify Strengths:* Identifying an employee's dominant strength themes and refining them with knowledge and skills. (Strengths are a person's ability to provide consistent, near-perfect performance in given activities.)
2. *The Right Fit:* Placing the right people in the right roles with the right managers.
3. *Great Managers:* Developing managers who will (a) opt for talent not simply experience, intelligence, or determination; (b) define the right outcomes, not the steps to get there; (c) focus on the person's strengths, not their weaknesses; and, (d) use the "Gallup Q12" (below) as a guide to understand and develop employees.
4. *Engaged Employees:* Developing employees so they can answer all the questions in the "Gallup Q12" (below) with strong affirmative responses.
5. *Engaged Customers:* Developing employees who engage customers to experience products r services in a superior fashion.
6. *Sustainable Growth:* Producing efforts that are metrically measurable such as revenue per store, revenue per product, or number of services used per customer.
7. *Real Profit Increase:* Producing sales growth tied directly to stock value.
8. *Stock Increase:* Sustaining profit increases that drive ongoing increases in stock value.

Further, this work offers organizational change agents 12 questions to tangibly measure the organization and its employees' mutual effectiveness. Referred to as the "Gallup Q12," the questions evoke satisfaction levels.

1. Do I know what is expected of me at work?
2. Do I have the materials and equipment I need to do my work right?
3. At work, do I have the opportunity to do what I do best every day?
4. In the last seven days, have I received recognition or praise for doing good work?
5. Does my supervisor, or someone at work, seem to care about me as a person?
6. Is there someone at work who encourages my development?
7. At work, do my opinions seem to count?
8. Does the mission/purpose of my company make me feel my job is important?
9. Are my co-workers committed to doing quality work?
10. Do I have a best friend at work?
11. In the last six months, has someone at work talked to me about my progress?

12. In the last year, have I had the opportunities at work to learn and grow?

Career consultant Nicholas Lore (Rockport Institute, 2003) states that only "…approximately ten percent of people report that they love their work." Yet, he notes that, "…when fit is optimal, workers find numerous indicators of increased job satisfaction, including experiencing work as a natural expression of one's talents and personality." Gallup's research indicates that as more of the Q12 questions are responded to as "strongly agree," work satisfaction grows, spurring on higher levels of organizational performance.

In a knowledge-based, technology-enhanced, globally-competitive workplace where success hinges on human capital, there is no more important issue than developing people to increase performance. Product innovation, timeliness, and quality earn customer satisfaction and loyalty—top company assets—achieved chiefly through developing human capital.

However, what does developing human capital entail? Becker, Huseld and Ulrich (2001) state that "…even when human resource professionals and senior line managers grasp this potential, many of them don't know how to take the first steps to realizing it" (p. 4). The most productive response seems to be dedication to developing people in three distinct ways:
- Presenting challenging tasks;
- Providing before, during and after feedback; and
- Supporting ongoing learning (Lombardo and Eichinger, 2002b).

Through helping organizations establish a career development culture, career specialists and change agents play pivotal roles in organizational and employee prosperity.

Developing Comprehensive Career Plans

"…Client presenting problems…are only a beginning point, and…as counseling unfolds, other problems emerge. Career issues frequently become personal-emotional issues, and family issues, and then career issues again" (Gysbers, Heppner, and Johnson, 2003, p.3).

Amundson (2003) points out that, "…most people come to counseling with life problems that do not fall neatly into the categories of career or personal: life just does not define itself that neatly" (p.16). However daunting the individual's needs appear, career development professionals assume responsibility for helping their clients create career plans.

Identifying Career Competencies

Emerging career development assumptions are challenging traditional beliefs (Feller, 2003) about the competencies needed for navigating a career and are fostering progressive policies and practices to improve high school-to-college-to-job transitions, as well as those adults transitioning to employment (Rosenbaum & Person, 2003). NOICC's "Career Development Competencies" (1996), the National Life/Work Center's "Blueprints for Work/Life Designs" (2001), and 40 developmental assets promoted by the Search Institute (1997), are all powerful tools to help determine and focus on needed client competencies. Spawned by business leaders, these newer competencies help clients prepare better for career choices and sustain career satisfaction.

Identifying Individual Strengths

"Strengths models" represent some of the more recent developments in career planning tools. Arguing that discovering and capitalizing on one's strength increases the potential of performance excellence as well as work success and satisfaction in life, strength models have become available commercially. The StrengthsFinder™, an on-line adult assessment within the framework *Now Discover Your Strengths* (Buckingham & Clifton, 2001), as well as its youth counterpart in *StrengthsQuest: Discover and Develop Your Strengths in Academics, Career, and Beyond* (Clifton and Anderson, 2001) help clients identify their top 5 of 34 strength themes. This feedback can serve as the foundation for goal setting and planning for change.

Lombardo and Eichinger (2002b) have identified 67 competencies, falling into six factors — Strategic Skills, Operating Skills, Courage, Energy and Drive, Organizational Positioning Skills, and Personal and Interpersonal Skills. Their work (2002a) also identifies 10 performance dimensions and 19 career inhibiters and stoppers, while proposing client competencies in positive and straight-forward language. Called the "Career Architect" (Lombardo & Eichinger, 2002a), in its simplest application, counselors ask clients to sort 67 cards into 3 roughly equal piles in response to the question, "What are my 22 highest, middle and lowest skills?" They find that the forced sorting, although sometimes resisted by clients, is critical for more accurate outcomes as people tend to be overly positive or negative without a forced-choice method.

Because self-assessments may be only partially accurate (people tend to be fairly accurate about their strengths and less so about their "soft" areas), it is recommended clients validate the card sort with others who know them well. Career specialists next review the competency sorts, arranging the cards into larger clusters and identifying themes in the highest and lowest skills. Once the skills have been rated, the system offers the counselor and client a map to which each of the skills is tied, thus helping the client tangibly "see" the relative importance of each skill in successfully mastering career competencies.

In our experiences with these instruments, we've found that clients are able to gain tremendous insights into previously undiscovered competencies and talents. Additionally, they are helped to understand why some tasks come more readily than others, and how they might compensate for those that are overused or more difficult to master. The concrete suggestions for competency enhancement, carefully couched in the most positive of terms, allow clients to appreciate their inherent value while negotiating their intrinsic challenges.

Developing Individual Competencies

Clients experience tension anytime a gap between their vision and their current situation exists. Feedback about a mistake, failing at something important are examples of instances where gaps and consequent tension surface. Handled constructively, such tension can be used to motivate clients to master competencies at higher levels of effectiveness. However, where and when it occurs is pivotal. Lombardo and Eichinger (2002a) state, "...the odds are that [tension leading to subsequent] development will be about 70% from on-the-job experience, working on tasks and problems; about 20% from feedback or working around good and bad examples...; and 10% from courses and reading" (p. v.).

Most tensions occur when career specialists are not present, meaning that they need to teach clients coping techniques and tools they can use outside of sessions. These skills allow clients to maximize these growth opportunities. Lombardo and Eichinger (2002a) give 10 "remedies" for overcoming skill weaknesses for each of the 67 competencies, 10 performance dimensions, and 19 career inhibiters/stoppers that counselors can share with clients. While it is expected that no client would or need to be good at all 67 competencies at a single point, the need for all competencies plays out over career lifetimes as positions, functions, and levels of responsibility change.

We believe that such systems offer tremendous resources to help clients enhance strengths, develop "middle skills" into strengths, remedy weaknesses, work on untested areas, or compensate for overused strengths. We strongly endorse Eichinger and Lombardo (2002b) argument: The secret of success is continuously learning to do what you don't know how to do.

Articulating Concrete Goals

Good counseling traits and strong working alliances are fundamental for successful counseling outcomes. Bordin (1979) suggests three essential parts for creating a relationship while creating career planning goals:

1. Agreement between the client and the counselor on the outcomes expected in counseling;
2. Agreement on the tasks involved to achieve the outcomes; and
3. Commitment from both the client and counselor on the importance of the outcomes and tasks.

In the *Career Counselor's Handbook*, Figler and Bolles (1999) list the following 12 key skills for helping clients move from presenting problems, through identifying competency needs, through creating development plans, to articulating goals and taking action:
1. *Clarifying content*—Restating the essence of the client's needs.
2. *Reflecting feeling*—Identifying and restating the emotional quality of the client's needs.
3. *Open-ended questioning*—Asking questions that encourage a wide range of possible responses.
4. *Identifying skills*—Naming specific areas of talent or strength revealed through past experiences.
5. *Clarifying values*—Identifying sources of enjoyment and satisfaction via a client's description of past activities and experiences.
6. *Value imaging*—Encouraging clients to envision possibilities through open-ended brainstorming, imaging, visualization, and fantasizing.
7. *Information giving*—Giving key job or career information, enabling clients to better understand the need for all parts of the counseling process.
8. *Role-playing*—Providing practice in roles clients may face.
9. Spot-checking—Asking for feedback to keep the process on track.
10. *Summarizing*—Collecting all the information clients have and reviewing it for purposes of moving forward.
11. *Task setting*—Asking clients to gather information or engage in experiences relevant to development objectives.
12. Establishing the Yes, Buts—Identifying main concerns, obstacles, or roadblocks standing in the way of development plans, remedies, or goals.

Setting Career Goals

Developing comprehensive career plans is an iterative process; clients start and stop, reframe, try out new thoughts, feelings, and behaviors as they explore options. Clients often have complicated issues beyond the counselor's control. Consider Harrington's (2003) "dual track model." In the initial meetings (Track 1), the counselor usually responds to client inquiries about career, self, job finding, and job preparation. These initial meetings set the stage for clients to begin reflecting on their chief motivating factors—life styles, life purpose and meaning, strengths, likes and dislikes, etc. As the counseling sessions "mature" (Track 2), clients are integrating self-knowledge with career information, making decisions based on an evolving self-concept, and matching personality type with work environments. Understanding that the client will undoubtedly move between the two tracks, counselors using the dual track model can keep focused on the overall goals, while allowing clients room for exploration and experimentation.

Another useful model for helping clients articulate their goals is Figler and Bolles' (1999) "1-2-3 career counseling" model. This model assumes that the themes of career counseling are captured in three questions:

1. What do you want to do?
2. What is stopping you from doing it?
3. What are you doing about it?

Understanding human development, particularly age and stage, gender, and diversity issues, helps counselors navigate the context within which goals are articulated. A useful acronym to guide goal selection, while keeping context in mind, is SMART. SMART proposes that goals should be kept Specific, Measurable, Achievable, Realistic, and Timebound. Creating goals within the SMART framework can aid the career development specialist in integrating the client's unique contextual issues into a manageable development plan.

Creating Action Plans

By looking inward, outward, and forward, clients create their action plans. Developing action plans is a dynamic, energy-driven process. For counselors, it usually means keeping clients motivated. One strategy that can encourage clients to continue their forward momentum is to find "allies of support," or those individuals who help keep them focused on completing the action plan tasks.

Often during the action planning stage, clients modify and expand their ideas and plans. Counselors can best assist their clients by helping them embrace ambiguity and avoid premature closure. Providing "homework" assignments and additional resources and information are ways to keep clients continuously engaged between sessions. Renewing client commitments, following timelines, focusing on the ultimate outcomes, and measuring progress concretely are all effective tools for ensuring success throughout the action plan phase.

Closing Considerations

Career development has never been more demanding. The workplace is more complex and has every indication of becoming more so. Workers are beleaguered by the new skills required of them. Organizations are in chaos as they grapple with where and how to remain competitive. The social contract between employees and employers is no longer operative.

Career development has never been more important. Many individuals are prepared to change their lifestyles, set development goals, or want help coping with job searches in workplaces that change faster than they adapt. Some land in jobs and lifestyles with little planning; many lack awareness of their skills, abilities, and interests, or have little experience making self-directed decisions. Several are motivated lifelong learners, seeking permission and encouragement to plan for a new life direction.

Commonly referred to as the "boomer population" in *Age Power: How the 21st Century Will Be Ruled by the New Old* (Dychtwald, 2000), this group presents career development issues differently. Career counselors are challenged to implement career planning interventions in more creative ways—weekend workshops or retreats, ongoing, on-site employee development trainings. Presenting engaging activities that help these clients capture insights into personal happiness, yet highlight the realities needed to attain their goals create new counseling opportunities.

Career development has never been more exciting. It attends to the very personal emotional domain of individuals on their lifelong journeys, searching for satisfaction and quality in every choice. Helping create and achieve these life stories, professionals are in a wider range of settings with greater variety in titles and training backgrounds. They are consistently driven to keep pace with rapid changes. The only constant—the number of individuals needing comprehensive career development plans will grow. As in the past, growth will spawn new and dynamic personal growth and development tools, strategies, and philosophies to nurture passion, identify potential, and honor the courageous choices of our clients.

Chapter Implications

- Assumptions under-girding career development are undergoing major shifts. To remain effective, career specialists, educational leaders, and organizational change agents will need to adapt their perceptions and skills accordingly.
- Planning careers is an iterative, lifelong, holistic activity throughout which individuals create and live their lives.
- Career development has a growing presence in organizations interested in developing and enhancing both corporate and individual purpose and meaning.
- Career development has moved beyond "something done at key decision points" with youth in search of a destination to a multi-disciplinary approach with varied techniques for clients of all ages.
- Many workers in search of career changes present unique challenges — valuing their personal time, finding expression and meaning in multiple outlets, questioning their life purpose, and seeking connections through spirituality. They want relevant career information succinctly and incisively. Challenging their assumptions about how to explore and grow demands a sense of creativity on the helper's part.
- Career development has emerged as a sociopolitical instrument, infusing economic vitality into communities, etching humanistic values into turbulent workplaces and enhancing personal freedom and organizational performance.

CHAPTER 8

Change Requires Agility and Intuition

"Speed demands greater use of intuition as the most important competitive weapon...[there's] little time for reflection, to think, to analyze, to go off and study things...[you're] compet[ing] with people willing to take chances...those standing back and relying on tools of the industrial age to make decisions will be left behind!"

V.P. Intel (from *Secrets of Silicon Valley*, 2001)

Isn't it ironic that the only constant in the known universe — change — is the one thing most consistently resisted by the majority of people? Yet, to experience success and meaningful lives, change is mandatory to keep us learning, excited about our potential, and competitive in the workplace.

We're including information on how people change to help counselors and career development professionals work most effectively with their students and clients. Following the precept that "forewarned is forearmed," we believe that, when people understand the range of reactions from others and themselves, they can stay focused and self-manage themselves more successfully. After speaking to change, we move to agility — the quintessential result of embracing change. We will also share our findings on the value of intuition, particularly how it can consciously and unconsciously affect our decision making and choices. A keen sense for the variables shaping the change process is the hallmark of a change agent moving an organization to higher performance, a career specialist getting the best out of clients, or an educational leader or counselor garnering the trust of the "forgotten half" of students.

Change—What Is It Really?

"At first I thought there would be common factors in [counseling strategies]. However, I realized that clients spend less than 1% of their waking hours in...sessions. ...Next, I noted that less than 10% of populations plagued by the major killers of our time (e.g., smoking, sedentary lifestyles, and unhealthy diets) ever seek professional

assistance. Given how few people actually participate in [counseling, my] search shifted from how do people change in [counseling] to how do people change, period."

James O. Prochaska, "How Do People Change, and How Can We Change to Help Many More People? In *The Heart & Soul of Change* (1999, p. 227)

Research shows that change is a process that evolves over time. How much time is uniquely individual. Change is highly personal and largely dependent on prevailing circumstances. Typically, it progresses through five stages: precontemplation, contemplation, preparation, action, maintenance, and termination (Prochaska, 1999).

1. *Precontemplation:* In this stage, people are not thinking of changing within the next six months. Reasons for remaining in this stage are multiple and include denial, defensiveness, no or misinformation. They typically are unmotivated and resistant to change. In the field of career development, precontemplation can be characterized by those individuals who are not necessarily satisfied by their current career, may be unhappy enough to possibly want to change, but are "settling for less." Generally, they underestimate the benefits of changing and overestimate the effort.

2. *Contemplation:* Contemplation is the stage wherein people intend to change within the next six months. Although they are aware of the benefits of changing, they may be disproportionately concerned about the cons, thus wallowing in ambivalence. It is still difficult for these individuals to actually change; they may remain stuck in "chronic" contemplation or ambivalence for some time. They are often characterized as "yes, buts."

3. *Preparation:* Those in this stage are ready to take action within the next month or so. They may have a plan or taken significant action within the past year. They are ready for intervention (though not necessarily anything long-term) and are open to new ideas. They have sufficient motivation to implement change and seek help doing so.

4. *Action:* People in this stage have made recent obvious lifestyle or career changes, have measured their progress, and evaluated their success. They are propelled by enthusiasm and a heightened sense of self-efficacy.

5. *Maintenance:* In this stage, people are working to continue their momentum. This final stage of change occurs when individuals have taken ownership of their behaviors, have modified them, and have practiced them sufficiently to become comfortable in

their use; in this sense the changes—both attitudinal and behavioral—are "second nature." During this stage, they may need periodic support to keep from losing their new beliefs and behaviors.

Generally, career development professionals form meaningful, often lasting relationships with their clients and students. As with any relationship, counseling techniques are eclipsed in importance by intra and interpersonal skills. What we learned when researching this chapter is just how important these relationship factors are to successful counseling outcomes. A comprehensive synthesis of therapy models, which include most of the techniques career professionals are taught and use in their sessions, revealed the following common factors and their percentage of contribution to successful change (Murphy, 1999).

- Client—40%; personal strengths, talents, resources, beliefs, social supports, and fortuitous events in the client's life.
- Relationship—30%; perceived empathy, acceptance, and warmth.
- Expectancy—15%; the client's hope and expectancy of change as a result of participating in the development process.
- Model/technique—15%; theoretical orientation and intervention techniques used by the practitioner.

We believe that these findings have promising implications for career development in that they can help us determine:

- Our effectiveness in building and maintaining the relationship;
- The factors and influences within or beyond our control;
- What may or may not be working and what adjustments are needed to strengthen the relationship; and
- The likelihood of achieving certain outcomes.

Client Factors

These are the most potent source of change. They are what clients bring with them to the career development process. They include such dimensions as their strengths, beliefs, values, skills, experiences, ability to enlist the help and support of others, potential for change, and desired changes that are already happening in their lives.

When counselors are able to identify and tap into these factors, results are dramatically enhanced. Practitioners can empower client assets by:

- Assessing the client's strengths and resources related to the desired outcomes;
- Asking clients about their beliefs about their desired outcomes; and
- Selecting strategies that are compatible with the client's beliefs

and values.

Relationship Factors

The second most important component in effective career counseling, relationship factors, are fundamentally a matter of personality and style. They include empathy, warmth, caring, genuineness, acceptance, and encouragement, and are judged solely by the client (Murphy, 1999). Clients report that the counselor-client partnership is best when their counselors:

- Accept the clients' goals at face value rather them challenging them to change them;
- Tailor tasks and suggestions to the client instead of asking the client to conform to the counselor's methodology;
- Collaborate with clients rather than dictate to them; and
- Explore material and options relevant to the client.

Expectancy Factors

When clients are demoralized, the counselor's job is considerably hampered. Clients entering the counseling relationship hopeful and optimistic about outcomes create an initial sanguine tone that typically prevails throughout the career development process. Counselors can activate hope and optimism by:

- Conveying an attitude of hope and possibility without minimizing obstacles or the difficulty of change; and
- Encouraging clients to focus on present and future possibilities instead of past problems or failures.

Learning the stages of change and recognizing where clients fall within the change process can make the difference between positive and negative counseling outcomes. Certainly who the client or student is has a dramatic impact on what is achieved through career development; however, career development professionals employing certain techniques can elicit more favorable client attributes.

Initiating Change—Changing Mind-Sets

More and more frequently, particularly in today's fast-paced workplace, changing minds and behaviors is important to both an organization's and an employee's well-being. How can change occur, especially when it means altering the culture—what the company believes and practices—of an organization? What can promote successful changes of this magnitude?

In their research, Lawson and Price (2003) synthesized four conditions for changing mind sets:

- A purpose to believe in;
- Reinforcement systems;
- The skills required for change; and
- Consistent role models.

A Purpose to Believe In

"Cognitive dissonance," a term coined by the Stanford social psychologist, Leon Festinger (1957), is the agitated mental state that occurs when people's beliefs are inconsistent with their actions. In his studies, Festinger noticed that people have an inherent need to eliminate cognitive dissonance by either changing their beliefs or their actions. The implication of his findings for initiating change is that when people believe in an overarching purpose, they will change their actions. Equally important, however, is that they also need to understand the specific role they play in promoting this purpose *and* believe that it is worthwhile for them to embrace.

Reinforcement Systems

For people to continue with their new actions, they must benefit in ways commensurate with their change efforts. Within organizations, this means that reporting structures, management and operational processes, and measurement procedures—setting targets, measuring performance, and giving financial and nonfinancial rewards—must be consistent with the new behaviors. Individuals must receive payoffs that encourage their ongoing labors; otherwise new behaviors will be replaced by older, more familiar ones.

The Skills Required for Change

Learning new behaviors is frequently difficult; we often make the mistake of expecting actions to change without teaching individuals the skills for making the changes. David Kolb (1984), a specialist in adult learning, developed his adult-learning cycle. Adults don't learn by merely listening; they must also:
- Absorb the information;
- Use it experimentally; and
- Integrate it with their existing knowledge.

This means that learning needs to be broken into pieces, with time between learning for people to reflect, experiment, and apply the new principles. Additionally, when people are given the opportunity to describe to others how they are adapting the new information to their circumstances, they learn more thoroughly.

Consistent Role Models

Benjamin Spock, the well-known pediatrician, insisted that consistent role models are the decisive factor in the development of children. Research shows that this remains true in most social circumstances, including work. People typically model their behaviors after those in positions of influence. To effect change within an organization, people of influence must "walk the talk." People in organizations also change relative to the groups with which they identify (not unlike teenagers!). Role modeling must consistently be confirmed by those around them if we expect individuals to change. To expect key groups to change, the change must be meaningful to them.

When they put their findings into practice, Lawson and Price (2003) noted significant cultural transformation across the organization. Comparing pre and post-test outcomes, they noted significant positive changes in the organization's emphasis on leadership development, achievement, teamwork, continuous improvement, and integrity.

Reframing – A Powerful Precursor to Change

Continuous improvement, building teams and learning from others requires the honoring of diverse talents and viewpoints. Changing perspectives through the reframing of how we understand others precedes most change, innovation, or adaptation.

Throughout our careers, we have worked with several change models in myriad settings with various clients. One model with which we are intimately familiar is *True Colors*™ . This system is based on a metaphor developed by Don Lowry in 1979 (see www.true-colors.com/about/index.htm and www.truecoloscareer.com for background on the evolvement of the concept). Its application to career development is well illustrated by Carolyn Kalil in her book, *Follow Your True Colors to the Work You Love*. Using colors to identify four distinct perspectives and personalities, *True Colors*™ promotes deeper understanding of interactions between self and others. *True Colors*™ encourages people to honor diversity by teaching ways of opening themselves to individual differences. Reframing our perspectives helps change negative beliefs and attitudes about human behaviors into positive ones. We're including a list of reframing examples as a tool for enhancing the change process (see Table 12). These examples offer clients the chance to see that they have choices in how they view and understand themselves, colleagues, and others who present unique perspectives.

Table 12. Reframing—Changing Negative Attitudes and Beliefs to Positive Ones

Negative	Positive	Negative	Positive
Snobbish	Intellectual	Irresponsible	Fun-loving
Arrogant	98% right	Flaky	Spontaneous
Not caring about others	Efficient	Wishy-washy	Flexible, adaptable
Unrealistic	Creative, visionary	Not serious	Carefree
Eccentric, weird	Original, unique	Disobeys rules	Creative problem solver
Ignoring people's values	Reasonable, rational	Unable to focus	Multi-tasker
Aloof, unfeeling	Calm	Manipulative	Good negotiator
Afraid to open up	Under control	Ignores details	Mover and shaker
Overly analytical	Precise	Rigid	Stable
Critical, faultfinding	Objective analysis	Controlling	Providing security
Heartless	Fact-based decisions	Dull, boring	Dependable
Overly emotional	Warm	Stubborn	Firm
A "bleeding heart"	Caring, compassionate	Opinionated	Have a perspective
Flaky	Spiritual	System-bound	Efficient
Hopelessly naïve	Idealistic	Unimaginative	Realistic
Too tender hearted	People person	Judgmental	Decisive

Table 12 cont.

Too "touchy-feely"	Unselfish	Uptight	Orderly, neat
Too nice	Affirming	Having own agenda	Organized
Smothering	Caretaker	Inflexible with time	Punctual
Soft	Sympathetic	End justifying means	Goal Oriented

Based on *True Colors*™ concepts and materials

The Magic of the Possible Self

We hear of it often, particularly in the sport's world—you're two strokes ahead of the leader; you're in a bunker on the 10th hole; you can see the pin; you know the perfect shot; now *visualize* yourself making this shot; now *visualize* yourself the winner. We seldom, however, hear of visualization in career development contexts. Seemingly, this is changing. Sandra Kerka (2003) in her work, *Possible Selves: Envisioning the Future,* speaks about envisioning possibilities as a powerful tool for career development. "Possible selves" represent individuals' ideas of what they might become, what they would like to become, and what they fear about becoming it (Markus & Nurius, 1986).

The "possible selves" concepts have been used with adolescents exploring career choices, adults in transition, and older adults adjusting to life in the knowledge workplace with very promising results (Kerka, 2003). Possible selves techniques include using imagery and visualization to create "behavioral blueprints" to help guide behavior toward what we might become and conquer fears preventing us from attaining our goals. In essence, the notion of possible selves reflects the influences of cognition and emotions on behavior ("If you can see it, you can become it"), as well as the ways significant others affect aspirations.

Learning Agility—Separating the Best From the Rest

"[What separates the successful executives from those whose careers derail]...is their agility in wresting meaning from experience. Successful executives are much more likely to have active and numerous learning strategies. They learn faster, gaining their lessons closer to on-the-spot, not because they are more intelligent, but because they have more learning skills and strategies that help them learn what to do when they don't know *what to do. They're also more open to what they don't know.*

Suppleness, adaptability, and flexibility—characteristics often touted as the essential ingredients of employment success—have been enhanced by the concept of learning agility. Learning agility inspires a myriad of behaviors such as the ability to think and respond thoughtfully almost instantaneously. Being able to say "Yes I can" when you really have no definitive plan in mind or operating from a basis of supreme self-confidence (not arrogance!) are not only traits of the Knowledge Nomad but signs that we are on top of our day. Knowing and using innate talents and gifts to excel, understanding where one fits in the overall scheme of things, seeking and accomplishing the new and unusual, and making every event an opportunity are ingredients seen in colleagues who help us grow.

Eichinger, Lombardo and Raymond (2004) defined learning agility and highlighted its importance in career success in their book *FYI For Talent Management* (2004). Through multi-year studies, they identified the primary characteristic—*learning agility* and its components—of successful employees. They've defined it as the ability to adjust, adapt, respond to, and be resourceful in the face of new conditions. It's performing well under first-time conditions; it's doing well what you've never done before. It's how well you adapt to the new and different.

What do people with high learning agility look like? Eichinger, Lombardo & Raymond, (2004, p. vii) propose they do four things well:

1. They are critical thinkers who examine problems carefully and make fresh connections.
2. They know themselves better and are able to handle tough people situations deftly.
3. They like to experiment and can deal with discomfort that surrounds change.
4. They deliver results in first-time situations through team building and personal drive.

They also break learning agility into four factors with 26 dimensions (see Table 13). With workplace change demanding these skills, career development professionals are well advised to promote the learning agility factors and characteristics to their clients and students.

Table 13. Learning Agility Factors and Characteristics

Agility Factor	Low Agility Characteristics	High Agility Characteristics
Mental	Trapped in present paradigms; uncomfortable with change, ambiguity; oriented to known solutions; may not be able to articulate the positions of others; may appear biased, non-objective or even arbitrary; focus on **what** rather than **why** or **how**	Oriented toward newness and complexity; mentally quick; seen as curious and inquisitive; delve deeply into problems, thoroughly analyzing them through contrasts, parallels, and searching for meaning; can get to the essence of issues quickly
People	Don't know themselves well; over or underestimate themselves and their skills; don't know their limits; mishandle situations they think they're handling well; lack insight into self and others; don't handle conflict well; inflexible; lack clarity; not constructive with others.	Self-managers in relationships; know themselves; open-minded to others; seek feedback and respond by personal change; seen as helpful, constructive even in disagreement; open to diverse people and viewpoints; clear in presenting viewpoints; relate to others well.
Change	Like things ordered and routine; uncomfortable with experimentation; may resist innovation; avoid conflict management; at extremes, seen as perfectionists who try to get everything just so; don't deal well with criticism.	Like to tinker with ideas and put them into practice; highly interested in ongoing improvement; cool under pressure; can handle the heat and consequences of being at the forefront of change efforts.
Results	Have trouble with first-time or difficult situations; have problems inspiring others; lack personal drive or presence; results suffer when something new is needed.	Deliver despite first-time or tough situations; build high-performing teams; demonstrate personal drive and adaptability.

Adapted from Eichinger, Lombardo & Raymond (2004).

Intuition—The Value of "Listening to Your Gut"

Howard Schultz had his eureka moment in Milan, Italy, when he realized that the leisurely caffeine-and-conversation cafe model would work in the United States. Market research would probably have warned him that Americans would never pay $3 for a cup of coffee. But Schultz didn't need research. He just knew he could turn coffee into a big business; he began literally shaking with excitement—and then started Starbucks (SBUX).

Related by Thomas Stewart in *Business 2.0* (November 2002)

Schultz' story carries an obvious moral: The most stellar decisions tend to come from the gut. Across the U.S., we tend to judge our feelings as non-rational. To hold merit, decisions are supposed to be carefully reasoned and based on tangible evidence. However, research done in economics, neurology, cognitive psychology, and other fields suggests that intuition, or instinct, or hunch, or learning without awareness is a real form of knowledge. In fact, according to Stewart (2002):

> ...it may be non rational, ineffable, and not always easy to get in touch with, but it can process more information on a more sophisticated level than most of us ever dreamed. Psychologists now say that far from being the opposite of effective decision-making, intuition is inseparable from it. Without it we couldn't decide anything at all. (p. 1).

There is even a term to describe people in close contact with their gut reactions—"high intuitives." How does one become more intuitive? While teaching skills for increasing one's ability to "listen to intuition" is not as straightforward as memorizing the periodic chart of elements, everyone can hone their instincts to some degree. Through his research and interviews with psychologists, Stewart (2002) offers the following guidelines:

- *Practice:* Practicing is most important. "Gut instinct is basically a form of pattern recognition," says Howard Gardner, a Harvard professor and psychologist. As you practice, your ability to recognize intuition grows. Examine your decisions, reconstructing your thinking, looking for their intuitive aspects, and noting their outcomes. Look for patterns- and don't let yourself be talked out of good ideas.
- *Learn to listen*: Most people fight the urge to listen to their gut. Flavia Cymbalista (the inspirational greeting card magnate) developed a decision-making approach based on a psychological technique called "focusing." She uses this technique to teach business people to find their "felt sense"—knowing something they can't articulate—and then listen to what the felt sense has to say.
- *Tell stories*: Fictionalizing a problem similar to a business school case can release imaginations. Dave Snowden, director of IBM's Cynefin Centre for Organisational Complexity in Wales, works with anti-terrorism experts in this way. He finds they think more creatively if he poses problems set in the American Civil War period. Another kind of story telling is what cognitive psychologist Gary Klein calls a "pre-mortem." Imagine that your project has failed and gather the team to assess what went wrong.
- *Breed gut thinkers*: Remove obstacles that prevent people from using their guts. High turnover rates are adverse to developing

deep expertise that sharpens intuition. Gut feelings are difficult to express, particularly in organizational contexts; encourage people to share their feelings.

Stewart (2002, p. 1) ends with what he refers to as the moral of his story: "To sharpen your intuitive thinking, you have to get out of your own way; to foster it among those around you, you have to get out of their way too." As we work to help clients change, become more agile, and trust their intuition, we need to respond more creatively. By dropping our own inhibitions, self-imposed mental barriers, and re-occurring patterns, we may enhance our intuition and find unanticipated opportunities for change as well.

Chapter Implications

- People resist change even when they know it's the only option. They can, however, be encouraged to change and supported throughout the change process.
- People move through a predictable sequence when changing behaviors.
- Large-scale change happens in steps; plan carefully before beginning any wholesale restructuring within an organization.
- Compliance and flexibility have been supplanted by "learning agility"—the ability to adjust, adapt, respond to, and be resourceful in the face of new, rapidly changing conditions.
- Learning agility can be mastered.
- Intuition is increasingly valued as an essential ingredient in decision making; it is particularly important to inspiring innovation.
- Trust intuition, articulate hunches, and encourage others to do the same.
- Career development professionals need to impart more divergent, nontraditional skills to their students and clients to help them gain a competitive edge.

CHAPTER 9

Living And Working In Search
of Significance

"You rarely have time for everything you want in this life,
so you need to make choices. And hopefully your choices
can come from a deep sense of who you are."

Fred Rogers
The World According to Mister Rogers (2003, p. 32)

Our economy is changing from a money economy to a satisfaction economy. This is not a recent trend; it has been happening for over two decades (Seligman, 2002). As you might imagine, when jobs are scarce, personal satisfaction carries less weight than when jobs are more abundant. The enticement of great riches after several demanding work years is losing its glamour for numerous reasons. Workers are asking questions like, "Does my work have to be so dissatisfying, dehumanizing, and hollow?" And, they are answering, "No." For career development professionals, this shift in worker motivation has implications for helping students and clients plan and meet career goals.

This chapter speaks to the heart and soul of career development - namely, helping our students and clients live with meaning and significance. We present our findings on what really matters to people and what they are looking for in work and life. Research suggests that worker satisfaction appears to be based largely on personal strengths. We discuss that relationship and workplace factors that can increase or decrease satisfaction. We've spoken about how the workplace is changing, and now we outline the leverage workers have when selecting employment and suggest ways employers can entice and keep workers.

More Meaningful Choices

Worldwide, people are exploring the meaning of their lives and connecting with their most deeply held values. Spirituality is becoming increasingly important as a cultural mainstay, prompting profound changes in attitudes and lifestyles. Individuals are less tolerant of the gap between what they believe in and how they live and are continually seeking ways to narrow it. Richard Eckersley, in his article, "A New World View Struggles to Emerge" (2004), believes that our universal goal is the same: "...to feel that our lives express who we are and that we are living in harmony with the values we claim to espouse" (p. 22).

There is a growing trend of post-materialism, the moving away from material wealth as defining self toward living a life of purpose and meaning through self-expression. As an example, a study completed in 2002 (as reported in Eckersley, 2004) found that 23 percent of Australians aged 30-59 voluntarily made long term decisions to downsize their lifestyles and earn less money. Their reason was quality of life. They wanted to spend more time with family, live healthier lifestyles, seek more balance, find greater fulfillment, and lead less materialistic and more environment friendly lives. Similar studies conducted throughout the world are reporting that approximately the same percentages of European and United States citizens are joining the new quality of life movement.

There is also a shift away from believing that our political and organizational leaders can lead us in our individual quests for meaning and significance. In light of the recent Enron, Tyco fiascos, growing national deficit, and the tax breaks highlighted in *Perfectly Legal: The Covert Campaign to Rig Our Tax System to Benefit the Super Rich and Cheat Everybody Else* (Johnston, 2003), many are losing faith in traditional institutions. When *The State of Working America 2004-05* (Mishel, Bernstein & Allegretto (2003) documents how the significant profits from productivity benefit owners rather than workers, can one blame hourly workers for not trusting corporations or government's ability to provide safety nets and social capital investments? More and more individuals, rather than expecting leaders to shape more desirable futures, are creating it for themselves by taking responsibility for the design of their personal, social, and planetary future. Rather than morality being imposed by legislation or regulation, we are realizing that only through our personal choices will we instill morality in our social structures and cultures (Hawken, Lovins, & Lovins, 1999).

In the U.S., we continue to experience dramatic cultural shifts. The three greatest consequences of industrialization—urbanization of society, institutionalization of work, and the demise of the nuclear family—appear to be reversing. U.S. Census Bureau reports of the 1990s reveal Americans migrating out of cities and suburbs into exurban and rural areas for the first time in the twentieth century. Information work is migrating from corporate to home offices. Growing numbers of baby boomers are saddled with both their debt-riddled, un- or underemployed adult children and their increasingly dependent aging parents, harkening back to the multigenerational, extended families of preindustrial times (Eckersley, 2004).

What Gives Workers Satisfaction?

Recently, the Gallup Organization published results from a multi-year study involving four million workers across the U.S. Using frequency of recognition and praise as the measures to help determine levels of worker satisfaction, they found that an estimated 22 million workers are disengaged, or extremely negative, in their workplaces. The costs to the U.S. economy are staggering—up to *$300 billion dollars* a year in lost productivity, and this is probably an underestimate since it doesn't reflect absence, illness, and other problems workers experience when disengaged from their work and their companies (Rath & Clifton, 2004). Other facts revealed through their study are also are telling.

- The number-one reason people leave their jobs is they don't feel appreciated.
- 65% of Americans received no recognition in the workplace last year.
- Negative employees can scare off *every* customer they interact with—forever.
- 9 out of 10 people say they are more productive when they're around positive people.
- Increasing positive emotions could lengthen life span by ten years.

Money Isn't the Answer

"Money can't buy happiness"
—Proverbial Saying

In the wealthiest nations throughout the world, personal satisfaction appears to be gaining momentum as an employment motivator. More and more studies are finding that matching individual values and purpose with working life is appreciably more important than tantalizing, but meaningless high salaries. Consider the findings from a world-wide study (Seligman, 2002) asking participants what gave them personal satisfaction.

Money did correlate with personal satisfaction, but only in those countries with lower purchasing power; and then it didn't matter as much as we might expect. The study found that in order to raise levels of happiness, changes to external circumstances were the strongest effects. Those external circumstances rating highest were:

- Living in a wealthy democracy, not in an impoverished dictatorship (strong effect);
- Getting married (robust effect);
- Acquiring a rich social network (robust effect);
- Avoiding negative events and negative emotion (moderate effect); and
- Getting religion (moderate effect).

As far as happiness and life satisfaction are concerned, one needn't try the following:
- Making more money (more materialistic people are less happy).
- Staying healthy (surprisingly, unless health deteriorated into permanent disabilities, health did not make a difference in happiness levels).
- Getting as much education as possible (no effect).
- Changing your race or moving to a sunnier climate (no effect).

The staying healthy and education findings in the study reported by Seligman (2002) certainly run counter to what other research states about happiness and well-being. In a study that tracked 237 Harvard graduates and 332 socially disadvantaged youth since 1937, George Vaillant (as reported in Cromie, 2004) and colleagues from Harvard University Services identified seven predictors that can lead to good physical and mental health at ages 70, 80 and 90. Education was among those predictors of what Vaillant termed "aging happy and well"; education was more important to health and happiness than money and prestige. Moreover, those study participants who lived longest and enjoyed life most were those who were in good physical and mental health.

All Work and No Play — No Way!

Excessive overtime is no longer as readily accepted as a condition of employment as it once was by either employers or employees. Excessive work hours contribute to the soaring medical costs of U.S. companies; and lack of sleep is now acknowledged as a physical health risk because it debilitates our immune systems (Pfeffer, 2004). Working while exhausted obviously causes mistakes, creating losses in overall performance levels as well as performance qualities. Individuals are now more prone to seek out companies and contracts that offer them the time to balance work and life to gain greater fulfillment.

Although we apparently are trying to balance work and life, we may have a ways to go. The October, 2004, cover story of *Fast Company*, "Still Believe in Work Balance...Forget It!", addresses the often illusive goal of balancing work and life. Apparently, we are still juggling speed, energy, ambition, family, and leisure. Honore's (2004) book, *In Praise of Slowness: How a Worldwide Movement is Challenging the Cult of Speed*, presents an alternative way to live that may perhaps help us capture greater fulfillment. Within it, Larry Dorsey, M.D., author of *Reinventing Medicine* (1999), states that:

> ...persuading people of the merits of slowing down is only the beginning, however. Decelerating will be a struggle until we rewrite the rules that govern almost every sphere of life—the economy, the workplace, urban design, education, medicine. This will take a canny mix of gentle persuasion, visionary leadership, tough legislation and international consensus...Collectively we know our lives are frantic, and we want to slow down. Individually, more of us are applying the brakes and find that our quality of life improves. (p. 279)

Robert Reich in his book, *Reason* (2004), coined the term "DINS"—"double income, no sex"—those families with two parent incomes struggling to raise families and make ends meet. Unfortunately, this trend has grown over the past few decades, chiefly because the proportion of married women in the workplace with children under six rose from below 20 percent in 1960 to over 60 percent by the late 1990s. We contend that as more families face quality of life issues—looking for meaning and significance – employers making conscientious efforts to help workers balance work and life will have the greatest competitive edge. Those who make it easier for women *and* men to have more job flexibility to attend to their young families and pay for family leave will be more and more attractive to skilled workers.

Leading with Our Strengths

After compiling several studies, we concluded that successful workers and workplaces have numerous commonalities, the majority of which revolve around individual strengths. Seligman (2002) uses the concept of "flow" (Csikszentmihalyi, 1991), which is based largely on personal strengths. He suggests:

- Flow is a positive emotion about the present with no conscious thought or feeling attached.
- Flow occurs when the challenges one faces mesh highly with one's abilities to meet them.
- The amount of flow workers experience on the job is directly proportionate to their level of satisfaction.
- Abilities include not just talents, but strengths and virtues as well.

To enhance "flow," Seligman (2002) suggests that:

- Workers identify their signature strengths.
- Workers choose work that allows them to use these strengths every day.
- Workers recraft their present positions to include more signature strengths.
- Employers choose employees whose signature strengths match their work responsibilities.
- Managers make room for their employees to recraft their work within the purview of company goals.

It's Not Your Father's World Anymore

In their book, *The War for Talent*, Michaels, Handfield-Jones, and Axelrod (2001) note how the workplace must change to attract and retain talent. They contend that many businesses continue to operate under old notions about employee value and worth, and consequently are losing talent to those organizations that are more employee-focused. In their work, they offer the old versus new business "realities" highlighting the leverage workers really have.

Increasingly, workers are letting their employers know that the "old" workplace realities won't work in eliciting their full engagement. In their survey report, *The Organizational Dance Card*, BlessingWhite (2004) report the results of their study of employee engagement. If organizations expect employees to rally to their purpose, they must heed employee needs. *Employees expect* (in descending order of importance):

- Adequate resources.
- Regular specific feedback.
- Greater clarity about what the organization expects.
- Development opportunities/training.
- A coach or mentor.
- Greater clarity about how what they do supports the organization's mission.
- Better communication with managers.
- Better relationships with co-workers.

BlessingWhite (2004) further concluded that what would most *improve workers' satisfaction* with their jobs (in descending order of importance) would be:

- More opportunity to do what they do best (again about strengths and talents).
- Career development opportunities.
- Greater clarity about how what they do supports the organization's mission.

- Improved cooperation among co-workers.
- Better relationship with manager(s).
- More challenging tasks.
- More say in how their work gets done.

The Old Reality	The New Reality
People need companies—people assume that companies control their welfare.	Companies need people—people understand that they are pivotal to company success; they control the companies' destinies.
Machines, capital, and geography are the competitive advantage—the more connected the organization is throughout the world, the greater the profitability.	Talented people are the competitive advantage—a company's only real competitive edge is the talent it is able to recruit and retain.
Better talent makes some difference—talent is important, but not as important as the latest technology or market positioning.	Better talent makes a huge difference—innovations are the single greatest corporate asset; those able to attract talent that can continually add value through their innovations are those who will compete most successfully.
Employees are loyal and jobs are secure—the job is for life; employees want the security the paternalistic corporation offers.	People are mobile and their commitment is short term—with the new social contract, workers are accustomed to working independently; their loyalty is to themselves and the perpetuation of their growth.
People accept the standard package they are offered—workers are satisfied with the standard health and retirement benefits typically offered.	People negotiate for much more—people are interested in benefits as such, but are really looking for significance and meaning in their career.

(Compiled from BlessingWhite, 2004; Eckersley, 2004; Michaels, Handfield-Jones & Axelrod, 2001; Reich, 2002).

What Organizations Can Do to Entice and Keep Talent

"The effective organization is still the one that recognizes that it must build a community of like-minded people who are on the same page, moving in the same direction, motivated to working together and who have a sense of being connected together in a worthwhile enterprise. That's what gives meaning to work and even to human existence."

Roger D'Aprix, Author and former communication leader at Xerox, Mercer Human Resource Consulting and Towers Perrin. *SCM* (Gorman, 2003, p. 16)

Many career development professionals help organizations establish programs to boost the likelihood of attracting and keeping employees. Although we spoke to organizational development more fully in Chapter 7, we include the following suggestions as they specifically focus on employee satisfaction in the workplace. The "Manager's Communication Model" (D'Aprix, as reported by Gorman, 2003) emphasizes the importance of all levels of leadership employing several essential strategies. Evidence indicates that when practiced they induce a climate of caring wherein employees feel valued and respected for who they are, as well as for their contributions. These strategies call for managers to:

- Ensure that every employee *understands his/her job responsibilities*. Answer the question "What's my job?" from the employee's perspective.
- Provide regular, consistent, constructive *performance feedback*. Continually address the employee's question "How am I doing?"
- Always answer employees' questions, "Does anyone care?" with a resounding "Yes." (Individuals *must know they matter*.)
- Help employees *understand the larger performance picture*. Timely updates on work unit objectives and results need to be relayed to answer the question, "How is my unit doing?"
- Ensure that every employee understands and is *aligned with the organization's vision, mission and values*. Answering the question, "Where are we heading?" ensures an appropriate point of departure for practicing this strategy.
- Be *committed to empowering* every employee. Continuously asking, "How can I help?" and garnering the resources to support the employees' answers are critical to employee satisfaction.
- Understand that success in the new workplace means *aligning the workers' self-interests with the interests of the enterprise*.

Also, in the BlessingWhite study (2004), they sought answers to the question, "How do you engage the hearts and minds of employees?" They found that to fully develop employee talents and engagement, organizations need to be ready to commit resources to certain strategies. Their bottom line conclusion: Employees want to do the work, but only when they have the emotional connection to their job; it's up to the organization to make that connection happen.

For organizations to encourage all-important employment engagement, BlessingWhite (2004) suggests that they:

- *Communicate and communicate more*. Each employee needs a deep understanding of an organization's strategy, values, and specific job priorities. Organizational goals need to be continually reinforced throughout all levels.

- *Focus leadership on the goals and the employees.* When senior leaders are seen as trustworthy, credible, and supportive, people are more likely to see the organization as a good place to work.
- *Reinforce personal success and alignment with the organization.* Encourage employee's talents; give them room to grow and responsibility to manage their growth. Ensure they have the necessary resources.
- *Build and maintain organizational pride.* Pride in the organization one works for is the foundation of pride in one's work. Emphasize organizational strength and find ways for employees to feel part of that strength.
- *Focus on customer satisfaction.* Employees feel more connected to an organization with a good reputation. Foster a positive reputation by committing to customer satisfaction.

The last strategies we'll share for helping workers find meaning in their workplaces come from the field of developmental psychology, most specifically positive psychology. Seemingly whimsical and simplistic at first blush, Rath and Clifton's (2004) *How Full Is Your Bucket?* actually blends research, science, and human experiential wisdom in their five strategies for more meaningful lives. When we read it, we immediately recognized its applicability to career and organizational development. They propose:
- *Strategy One*—Prevent bucket dipping. This refers to how we can create positive or negative feelings in our and others' lives. We empty, or dip from, buckets through negativity, as when we withhold all positive emotional support. We fill buckets when we create positive emotion. In organizations, this is chiefly accomplished through recognition and praise.
- *Strategy Two*—Shine a light on what is right. Rather than focusing on what is wrong, look at what is right; point out positive attributes at every opportunity; deal with problems constructively.
- *Strategy Three*—Make best friends. Interestingly, people with "best friends" at work have better safety records, receive higher customer satisfaction scores, and demonstrate increased workplace productivity. Encourage such alliances among your colleagues.
- *Strategy Four*—Give unexpectedly. People would rather receive unexpected than expected gifts. Don't wait until review time to share achievements Gifts don't have to be tangible; they can be trust or responsibility. Smile frequently.
- *Strategy Five*—Reverse the golden rule. Practice the rule, "Do unto others as they would have you do unto them," by taking the

time to learn about others - what makes them feel good; what motivates them. We're not alike in how we like our buckets filled.

How to Help Students and Clients Leverage Resources to Dispel Career Development Myths

As career development professionals, we typically try to help our students and clients discover their strengths, talents, interests, and life purpose and then help them pursue careers that engage their discoveries. We think, however, that many of us haven't fully understood how unplanned events influence careers. In their book, *Luck is No Accident*, Krumboltz and Levin (2004) introduce their views on "...making the most of happenstance in...life and careers." We've distilled their thoughts—chiefly myths about career development (see Table 14)—in this chapter because we recognize their practical value in helping individuals adapt to life's changes.

Table 14. Dispelling Common Life and Career Planning Myths

Myth	Reality
• Don't let unexpected events disrupt your plans.	• Make the most of unplanned events—take advantage of unexpected disappoints; convert frustrations into opportunities; work with what you've got.
• Choose a career goal as soon as possible.	• Always keep your options open—avoid tunnel vision; react to pressure with an open-mind; liberate yourself from unrealistic expectations; respond positively to challenging questions.
• Do all you can to make your "dream" come true.	• Wake up—before your "dream" comes true—when dreams fail, move on to something else; don't stick with a bad choice; test your dream one step at a time; open yourself to other alternatives.
• Take action only when you are sure of the outcome.	• Try it—even without knowing the outcome—take risks likely to pay off; be prepared for unexpected opportunities; take risks that may fail or with unknown outcomes; assume your interests will change.

Table 14 cont.

• Avoid making mistakes.	• Go ahead and make mistakes—make use of your and other's mistakes; recognize that chance plays a part in every decision; react to mistakes constructively; get on with your life.
• Wait for a lucky break.	• Take action to create your own luck —realize the future starts right now; take advantage of timely opportunities; ask for what you want; don't let self-doubt keep you from trying; persist in the face of rejection.
• Go for a job only if you have all the skills.	• Go for the job—then learn the skills—never "complete" your education; make every job a learning experience; use the skills learned in one job to qualify for the next; learn what you enjoy from your experiences; treat obstacles to learning as challenges.
• Put your career first.	• Enjoy yourself—the good life is a balanced life—put yourself in charge of creating a satisfying life; be all you can be.
• Always hold on to your beliefs.	• Overcome self-sabotage—you can change your career regardless of what you've done in the past; failure is a normal part of life and learning, not a disaster; develop helpful beliefs.
• Believe that luck is just an accident.	• Remember that luck is no accident— engaging in a variety of activities will help you discover what you like and dislike; you can create your own unplanned luck events by extending yourself; remember to always learn, always try, and always wonder.

(Adapted from Krumboltz & Levin, 2004)

Well-Being and Policy Implications

As career development professionals, one of our greatest (and sometimes most rewarding!) tasks is guiding educational and corporate policies. The shift in worker attitudes and lifestyles away from materialism to human interests and values has very provocative policy implications. To reflect Americas' changing cultural values with their obvious impact on workplaces, policy decisions at the organizational, corporate, and governmental levels should be more heavily influenced by "well-being"—

people's evaluations and feelings about their lives. In their work, *Beyond Money*, Diener and Seligman (2004) contend that economic indicators omit, limit, and even mislead our understanding about what society values. Because well-being provides information beyond that of strictly economic measures, they posit that well-being indicators should be included in economic growth evaluations. For example, although economic output has risen steeply over the past decades, there has been no rise in life satisfaction during this period; and there has been a substantial increase in depression and distrust. Now that most Americans have moved well beyond the fulfillment of basic needs and are growing wealthier, differences in well-being are less frequently ascribed to income and more frequently about social relationships and enjoyment in the workplace. Non-economic predictors of societal well-being include social capital, democratic governance, and human rights. In the workplace, non-economic factors influence work satisfaction and profitability.

Even if motives are chiefly based on profit-making, policy should still mirror worker and societal well-being. Desirable economic outcomes are often caused by well-being rather than the other way around. People reporting high well-being earn higher incomes and perform better at work than those with low well-being. Happy workers are better organizational citizens, meaning they support others in their efforts, as well as promote corporate success. Those high in well-being get along better with others, making better team members and leaders. Although the relationship is not understood, well-being is related to health and longevity (Diener & Seligman, 2004).

We need not belabor the relationship between economic and social well-being and productivity. Well-being and its benefits to healthy social relationships and institutions are self-evident. In our conversations about policy, we need to remember that well-being is not only valuable because it feels good, but also is valuable because it has wide-spread beneficial consequences across all of life's aspects.

Closing Thoughts

We're all looking for deeper meaning in our lives. Most of us have experienced the joy and anguish of honest self-reflection, and research supports that we're positioned to do it even more.   Across the world, congruence among all aspects of how we live our lives is the quest of more and more of us. We're not willing to settle for the hollow promises of materialism as an end in itself. We want to reap the rewards of meaningful self-expression. We've watched the consequences of our small-town markets growing into global economies, reducing the human connections that once provided support within our communities. We've grown detached from one another, making it easier to ignore one another's pain and the prevalence of gratuitous violence. We're literally yearning for a "better way" and increasingly determined to find it. We're learning that this life is not a dress rehearsal—it's the real show.

What are we concluding in our quest for significance? People matter most, things less so. We're beginning to measure successful lives by how we've lived, what we've contributed, and who we've helped, rather than what we have. We're moving away from isolating self-centeredness toward identifying ourselves as global citizens, responsible to the worldwide community. We're no longer asking ourselves to be the best *in* the world, but rather to be the best *for* the world (Jones, n.d.). Achieving significance has become our beacon. While success matters, seeking significance is a more inspiring and guiding principle from which to complete one's journey.

Chapter Implications

- Greater significance is attained by using our signature strengths daily and in all life roles.
- Organizations are challenged now more than ever to understand the very nature of individual self-fulfillment; that is their only real attraction for workers.
- One resource that the competition cannot duplicate is an organization's talent pool.
- We are who we create; we must use every opportunity to recreate ourselves.
- The questions we need to ask ourselves throughout our lives are increasingly more complex and difficult to answer. The answers, however, are the keys to living meaningful, fulfilling—significant—lives.

CHAPTER 10

Courageous Choices

"Thinking of choices...is another way of looking at the stands we take, the friends and enemies we keep. Our choices guide our journey. Choices are part of our stewardship of life: What shall we promise? What do we owe? What may I keep? What must I abandon?"

Max DePree
Leading Without Power (p. 153)

Throughout this book, we've spoken about the overarching forces such as globalization, widespread technology, connectivity, shifting values about money, time, personal satisfaction, and the alignment of work and personal meaning. We've noted the changes that need to occur in organizations and the questions educational leaders and change agents must ask to shift from a focus on discrete subject matter toward the more sophisticated contextual, interdisciplinary approach needed for adaptation throughout one's career at home, school, and work. We've noted the importance of teaching democracy in schools to enhance one's ability to live in our altering society and, most importantly, how to honor differences and change as opportunities for personal learning and growth.

We've seen how workplace skill expectations have changed and created the need for not just flexible workers but agile workers. Acceptance that knowledge is the most competitive edge is growing worldwide. Understanding that traits of the "Knowledge Nomads" are necessary for becoming the quintessential present and future workers is helpful to students as well as anyone considered "nervously employed." We've presented findings on sweeping global changes and the impact on cultural identities that void the social contract between employer and employee, escalating the number of the "Nervously Employed" and challenging traditional social structures.

In this final chapter, we present information on what career development professionals need to know to foster the healthy development of a nation and global community. Initially, we analyze choices—

particularly because we seldom take the time to reflect on the influence of our choices on how we live. Interestingly, we discovered the cost of having so many choices, resulting in what Barry Schwartz (2004) refers to as the "tyranny of choice." We'll speak to the implications of what David Pearce Snyder (2004) refers to as the "five meta-trends changing the world." We offer greater detail about our changing responsibilities as global citizens and what we might expect to see over the next few decades. We'll end with what we believe career development professionals need to understand to advocate for relevant career development policy and courageous choices.

We'll talk about the politics surrounding these sweeping global changes, not in the belief that we have the only or right views, but because politics *cannot* be separated from other parts of our lives. Politics imbue all facets of living and we offer ways to consider shaping these political forces in search of a "kinder, gentler world" (Stephens, 2002) so that we and our children can realize productive, meaningful, significant lives.

It is our hope that by synthesizing information throughout this book we've offered ideas to ponder and perhaps guide. To the degree this supports a more informed, deliberate, thoughtful career development professional, only time will tell. Ultimately, we hope this material fans the fires of individual strength and growth, leading to more *courageous choice making*.

The Importance of Choices

Essentially, our choices create our lives. They give birth to our purposes and goals. They move us into action, and our actions form our core. Through our choices, we decide how to spend our time and make ourselves accountable as we invent our tomorrow. Our choices make things happen. Circumstances fall into place, and the information and resources we need appear. Our lives work to the degree that we make choices that close the gap between expectations and experiences. Choices help us learn what we want and how to confront challenges before us. When one choice no longer sparks enthusiasm or moves us to act, then it's time to create a new choice that's more in tune with what we desire.

Our smallest choices can be as powerful and far-reaching as our boldest ones. The words we use in conversations with friends and the promises we keep that define our integrity and shape our legacy are all choices we may not realize we're making. We can't make every choice thoughtfully; time simply doesn't allow it. We can, however, make those choices about relationships, health promotion, and how we spend time to align with our purpose. They are, after all, the choices that ultimately determine who we become.

As career development professionals, we are in the business of nurturing passion, identifying potential, and honoring courage in choice-making. Our clients and students look to us as the "choice experts" in helping them create and attain meaningful lives. It appears, however, that for many our expertise may have its limitations as too much freedom in choice making can actually cloud decision-making. We're including the following information because we think it is critical to understand the pitfalls of having so many choices.

Too Many Choices?

We live in a world of abundance. U.S. citizens, the wealthiest (materially), in the world, are flooded with choices from the cars we buy, to the books we read, to the beds we sleep in. With affluence, we have the means to ponder and act on more choices. Yet, are increased options and their rewards making us happy?

The lessons of Economics 101 include one axiom that continually holds true. There is a point in material wealth when the satisfaction derived from purchases of goods and services begins to diminish. In fact, after this point (the point of diminishing returns), there is an *inverse* relationship between the quantity of material goods and consumer satisfaction. In other words, after a certain point; the more stuff you have, the less you enjoy it!

In his article, "The Tyranny of Choice," appearing in the *Chronicle of Higher Education,* Barry Schwartz (2004) notes that three recently published books from authors of three different disciplines—psychology, political science, and journalism—concluded that the growth of material affluence has *not* increased subjective well-being. In fact, people seem to be experiencing a decrease in well-being. Schwartz (2004) cites the following statistics:

- In the last 30 years, there was a 5% decline in the number of Americans describing themselves as "very happy" (that translates to 14 million fewer very happy people).
- The rate of serious clinical depression has more than tripled over the last two generations and increased by a factor of 10 from 1900 to 2000.
- Suicide rates are up in almost every developed country.
- Serious depression and suicide rates are the highest they've ever been among younger and younger people.

Schwartz (2004) contends that our current plethora of choices may contribute to our declines in general well-being. Having too much freedom with too many choices is a major source of stress, uncertainty, anxiety, and deep unhappiness. Greater choice *increases*:

- **Information gathering**. Gathering information used to be fairly straightforward – we'd make decisions based on lists of pros and cons, the opinions of others, and some outside research. Because we have so many options from which to choose, making conscientious choices is now about wading through mounds of data.

- **Likelihood of regret**. With all the available options, how does one ever know that the choice is the right one?
- **Avoidance of decision-making**. Anticipating that they will regret their choices, people often postpone making any decision at all.
- **Feelings of missed opportunities**. As they weigh the pros and cons of all their options; with all the choices and their accompanying data, people feel that no choice they make will capture everything they want.
- **Unrealistic expectations**. When people do settle on a choice, they overestimate how good the choice should be.
- **Self blame**. Decision makers are more likely to blame themselves when choices fail to meet their expectations (even when expectations are unreasonable).

To diminish the "tyranny of choice," he suggests that we delineate options and structure those we do offer, particularly to our children and young adults. He encourages us to understand that too many choices will often result in individuals making *no* choice at all.

The Global Community

We're including a discussion on the global community because it is what we are becoming; and, as such, influences our choices—profoundly. Throughout world history, we've watched the confluence of demographic, economic, and technological trends change lives forever. Current meta-trends are revolutionizing our globe in ways that we can only begin to imagine, much less comprehend. We found David Pearce Snyder's (2004) work a great point of departure for discussing these meta-trends as he synthesized well the sentiments of several futurists and other scholars (cf., de Soto, 2000; Dobbs, 2004; Hornstein, 2003; Thurow, 1999).

Trend 1—Cultural Modernization
Many underdeveloped countries with cultures that traditionally value authority, filial obedience, and self-discipline are undergoing astonishing transformations. Their youth are adopting more and more Western mores—manner of dress, choices of food and music; and most troublesome to those upholding the status quo, accepting Western thoughts. Yet despite the proliferation of terrorism (the outgrowth of those defending tradition), numerous social indicators signify cultural modernization is gaining ground

even in the most radical countries. Their average education levels for both men and women are growing; their percentage of women in the salaried workforce is rising; and their percentage of the population living in urban areas is increasing. Other indicators of cultural modernization, such as the percentage of salaried workers versus those self-employed and the percentage of GDP spent on institutionalized socioeconomic support services (insurance, pension, social security, civil law courts, worker's compensation, unemployment benefits, and welfare), also suggest cultural modernization. The primary measure of cultural modernization is declining birthrates. Countries like China and India report birth rates consistent with those of developed countries for people living in cities; birth rates remain high for those living in the country (Snyder, 2004).

Trend 2—Economic Globalization

Economic globalization as we've noted before is a double-edged sword. Proponents point to its long-term potential to raise living standards and reduce the costs of goods and services for people everywhere. Critics cite the short-term marketplace consequences of free trade—workers and businesses in both developed and developing nations facing potentially insurmountable competition. Despite where one stands on the issue, globalization is currently moving the world in some alarming directions. Wages are increasing for workers in developing nations, while depressing wages for comparable work in mature industrial economies. Workers in developed nations must now perform *incomparable* work, either in productivity or in superior products to earn more than those in the developing countries. And, while the trend toward economic globalization continues, the short-term disruption of local domestic employment means that global trade will remain an ongoing political issue.

Trend 3—Universal Connectivity

Connectivity, already exponentially enhancing communication across the world, will be accelerated when phones, cell phones, and other wireless telecom media are integrated with the Internet. By 2010, *all* long distance calls, and a third of all local calls, will be made via the Internet. Eighty to 90 percent of Internet access will be made from Web-enabled phones, PDAs, and wireless laptops. One-third of the world's population—two *billion* people—will have access to the Internet, primarily via Web-enabled telephones (Snyder, 2004). The Internet will be *the* Information Highway. There will be an increased emphasis on flexible employment, distance collaboration, and outsourcing within and outside of countries. Because of its global reach, the Internet will fashion a global consumer culture, frequented by the first global youth peer culture. "By 2010, we will truly be living in a global village, and cyberspace will be the town square" (Snyder,

2004, p. 25).

Trend 4—Transactional Transparency

Secrecy breeds corruption and disbelief, or so goes growing sentiment. Across the globe, we're becoming less charitable in our views of corporate and government deceit. There is a heightened worldwide consensus that all enterprises should reveal their principal transactions and decisions to the public. Interestingly, this comes during a time when most business management schools have dropped all ethics courses and business professors routinely preach that government regulation thwarts the efficiency of the marketplace (Snyder, 2004).

The global marketplace is increasingly demanding that corporations assume transparency protocols for the private sector. Not surprisingly, corporate and government leaders worldwide are lobbying hard against transparency mandates. However, consumer pressure for corporate integrity is gaining momentum. A recent study (Snyder, 2004) found that the majority of consumers are willing to use their individual power to punish those companies that do not share their values. Additionally, we're more and more aware of the consequences of human interaction with the environment. Across the world, citizens are convinced that sustaining our planet is crucial to a successful modern global economy. Total transparency is seen as one way of keeping sustainability in our uppermost thoughts.

Trend 5—Social Adaptation

Cultural modernization forces - particularly educational, urban and institutional – are impelling fundamental societal changes in both developed and developing nations. In the developed countries, citizens are less reliant on their leaders for guidance, adopting and using their own self-regulating tenets.

During the next decade, automated information will dramatically reduce paperwork. Outsourcing both inside and outside of the country will eliminate millions of U.S. middle-income jobs, forcing couples to work two lower-paying/lower-skill jobs to replace lost income. Identifying multiple sources of income becomes a common and strategic goal. Traditional concepts of family and work may change—more older workers may opt to work longer; husbands may stay at home when wives make more money; and adult children may move back home after college or divorce to save money and provide appropriate caregiving for their children.

As societies acclimatize to these meta-trends, new realities will materialize and create further changes in institutional environments. Intended and unintended outcomes of transformations will further rock our known human experiences. Yet, as these trends and their accompanying challenges evolve, many will adapt and prosper. Human adaptability and resilience may be stretched to their full capacity, and many will ultimately surface with a sense of satisfaction and well being.

"A Kinder, Gentler World"

In his *Futurist* article, Gene Stephens (2002) asks, "How can we create a kinder, gentler world?" He offers a twelve-step program for creating societies that trust more and hate less. We're including our translation of his twelve steps because we believe that in our roles as career development professionals and citizens we're responsible for understanding the importance of global citizenry to career and life choices. Stephens' (2002) 12 steps include:

1. *Embrace the global village.* We're in touch globally through accelerating connectivity. But, do we share the same ideals? Do we need to share the same ideals? What if we viewed "globality" differently? What if, rather than insisting we remain distinct from one another so as not to threaten our identities, we looked at our differences as opportunities to create a richer global society comprised of the best of many cultures?

2. *Recognize our homogeneity.* Anthropology tells us that we are all descendants of one human. Race, ethnic, and physical differences are not *true* distinguishing characteristics. They don't separate people—only culture does that. What if we redefined social systems to embrace others regardless of color and other apparent physical differences? Social systems are learned behaviors and can be changed, albeit not always easily.

3. *Celebrate diversity.* What if preserving and celebrating our unique, diverse heritages nourished our hearts? What if tolerance were taught and practiced? Do we not value our own identities? If so, don't we need to allow others to as well?

4. *Reject harming others in the name of religion.* Throughout recorded history, we have killed each other in the "name of God." What if we dropped the idea that "my God/gods is/are better than your God/gods?" After all, *none* of the worlds' foremost religions teaches humans to kill one another in their name.

5. *Eradicate violence at its roots.* What if we believed that violence had no place among truly civilized people? Violence is not essential to human well-being; it is not inherited – it is learned. Violence begets violence; peace begets peace.

6. *Stop perpetuating fear.* Although fear embeds life in many countries, what role do the media play in its perpetuation? We're all diminished through fear. Wouldn't we be better off if we looked toward hope?

7. *Seek justice, not retribution.* Hasn't history taught us that revenge is not justice? Locking up those convicted of crimes punishes taxpayers more than anyone else. We've seen rising crime rates almost universally. Do penal systems really protect society? What if we taught peace and conflict resolution skills, rather than war and punishment?

8. *Adopt peace.* Does anyone really *win* a war? Doesn't everyone have some degree of contribution in conflicts? Might we be better off if we looked for common ground and sought compromise in wrongdoings? If we look for ways for everyone to win, we just might gain world peace.

9. *Judge success by benefit to humanity.* I (Judy) remember reading an interview of Tom Selleck, who at the time was the chief actor in the highly successful television series, "Magnum PI." I don't recall the exact words, but I keenly remember its sentiment. The interviewer posed a question to Selleck about how it felt to be successful, and Selleck responded with words to the effect, "...what success? I didn't find a cure for cancer." What if success was measured in terms of contribution to the "greater good"? We know that the more "things we have," the less we enjoy any of them; and psychologists have learned that we derive our greatest satisfaction when we add benefit to humanity. What if our current standard of material wealth and money no longer defined success and was replaced instead by responsibility and contribution to the global good?

10. *Enjoy altruism.* Some of the deepest rewards to ourselves come from our anonymous acts toward and gifts to others. What if we taught our youth the joys of altruism and then practiced it ourselves?

11. *Appeal to the good in people.* People have the aptitude for ineffable goodness. We're taught through conditioning and reinforcement what to value, what to practice, and what to believe. What if we rewarded only acceptable behaviors and reinforced those values that make positive differences in lives?

12. *Rethink and reinforce the "golden rule."* Although we've covered this principle earlier in the book, it's important enough to repeat. This precept modifies the golden rule, "Do unto others as you would have them do unto you" (Christianity); or "What is hateful to you, do not do to your fellow man" (Judaism); or "No one of you is a believer until he desires for his brother that which he desires for himself" (Islam); or "Hurt not others in ways that you yourself would find hurtful" (Buddhism); to "Do unto others as they would have you do unto them." This axiom respects

individual and cultural differences and perpetuates compassion and empathy among people.

Globality—An Expanded Definition

We're all familiar with the term "globality." In most of today's discussions, globality typically equates with internationalism—a policy of political and economic cooperation among nations as well as an attitude favoring such a policy. America expresses its globality through international corporations (those domiciled in more than one country), international trade agreements, and foreign aid, to note a few examples. With the mounting deliberations on global citizenry and its place in globality, we believe that our current emphasis on "economic globality" is too narrow a perspective. We suggest that we expand the definition of globality to one more amenable to cultivating productive global relationships.

In our view, globality would emphasize human values and interests. Globality would encourage citizens of every country to understand that they must work toward setting and achieving not only national goals and priorities, but also international goals and priorities. More importantly, these national and international goals and priorities must *respect, honor, and subsume* the cultural ideologies and idiosyncrasies of every interacting country. Globality would recognize that the *functional* aspects of mutually determined and followed guidelines and regulations are not as important as their *human* aspects; and all human aspects would respect the feelings, thoughts, attitudes, beliefs, and values of all the global cultures.

In our view, globality transcends, not necessarily eliminates, those international alliances constructed by governments interested in securing and maintaining peace during and after war times. Globality assumes that world peace is the ultimate prize and world prosperity is the definitive criterion. Globality expects its citizens to proactively illuminate and participate in the resolution of common issues and problems in ways that are mutually beneficial.

Globality insists that we accept the mantle of global citizenry willingly, despite knowing that wearing this mantle means assuming as yet undiscovered responsibilities. Globality believes strongly that each and every citizen plays a role in shaping solutions for worldwide problems. Globality realizes that other countries may not yet embrace the same globality ideals, yet we're willing to champion our cause—we're committed to making the necessary courageous choices.

Our expanded concept of globality was not derived capriciously, and we found history was our greatest informant. We recalled the destiny of past empires that used their resources to dominate other countries and subsequently crumbled, leaving legacies of bitterness behind. We've seen countries wherein others have imposed their cultures, resulting in deep-seated hate and terrorism toward those countries. We've learned that the only real way to use power is to help others find their answers themselves, and then help them garner the resources to actualize their plans. In true globality, we know without a doubt that the fate of one is the fate of all. We pledge allegiance to country, and fidelity to the world.

Courageous Choices

Courage matters more than we may think. Without courage, our convictions remain illusive, private thoughts, of no benefit to ourselves or others. Without courage, we won't speak out against human abuses, oppression, or privilege, or make choices based on principle. Confronting ourselves with internal dissension or assuming responsibility for rectifying injustice takes courage. We can't experience our potential or pursue our passions without courage.

Scholars and leaders alike insist that courage is the essential human quality on which all other virtues are constructed. Courage is the moment wherein we confront our fears, connect our heart with our actions, and do what must be done despite what we might judge to be negative consequences. It's when our values and emotions align, compelling us to do what we know without doubt we must do. Courage is about heart; it's not about the brain. Courage involves the gut. It's going ahead and taking action, even though we're not sure of the results. Courage knows that risk is one of the key attributes of meaningful growth.

Can career development professionals learn to be courageous? According to Michael Useem (2004) of the Wharton School of Business at the University of Pennsylvania, we can. He suggests that by (a) preparing ourselves for future courageous actions by analyzing the outcomes of our decisions and learning what we might have done differently and (b) putting ourselves in situations that move us out of our comfort zones, we can react more productively and courageously under duress.

With globalization, accelerated technology, increased demands for learning, and a sense of exhaustion, more courageous choices are demanded of us. Yet, we find that America appears to be experiencing a courage scarcity. We tolerate corporate CEOs receiving multi-million dollar bonuses from companies *laying off* thousands of workers. We "spanked" energy trader's hands when we discovered the extent of their price gouging during California's energy crisis. Our sports' "heroes" are forgiven their flagrant acts of gratuitous violence ("It's just part of the game") toward each other. We insist on democratic practices from other countries, but don't always practice them ourselves. We have access to so many rich information sources, but too often defer to "talk radio" that gives voice to ignorance more than thoughtful discussion. We blame others for our failures, and seldom assume responsibility for correcting past wrongs. As a society, we have diminished personal accountability, integrity, and moral will.

Repaving the High Road

> "The true democracy, living and growing and inspriting…will not condemn those whose devotion to principle leads them to unpopular courses, but will reward courage, respect honor, and ultimately recognize right."

John F. Kennedy
http://www.jfkcontest.org/

As career development professionals, empowering others is our greatest contribution. When we encourage our clients and students to ask courageous questions, confront their fears, and make the tough choices, their quest for meaningful lives will not end. They are the ones who can insist on a society based on morality and leaders who operate organizations with transparency and integrity. They are the ones who can create the globality we envision.

We close this book with a template for creating and living courageous lives, lives that are firmly rooted in democratic principles and reflect personal accountability, integrity, ethics and compassion. We are convinced that if we introduce this template to our students and clients, they will be well on their way not only to meaningful careers, but also to fulfilling lives. Our suggestions cultivate the beliefs and behaviors of "Knowledge Nomads" and help those "Nervously Employed" overcome their fears and resume control of their careers. We are aware that not everyone chooses to be a "Knowledge Nomad," despite the evidence supporting their increasing status as the newest global worker. We would suggest, however, that those pondering their present and future careers at least consider the benefits such workers reap. With their skills and acumen, "Knowledge Nomads" may be in the enviable position of unlimited employment opportunities that resonate with their core values and goals.

Courageous career choices begin with courageous individuals. Individual maturity, belief systems, strengths, experiences, support systems, and so on are the foundation on which all decisions are built. Although career development cannot address all of these far-reaching, personal dimensions, the field can assist individual development by fostering certain behaviors, attitudes, and practices. The following template offers ways for career development professionals to help students and clients erect a solid personal foundation.

For ease of presentation, we've divided the template into two sections.

However, we realize that this division could be misleading by implying that a separation of what one does in one aspect of life does not necessarily influence other aspects. Nothing, however, could be further from the truth. We believe that the ideas of both sections are inextricably linked. Without a strong sense of self and purpose, the likelihood of a meaningful career is appreciably weakened.

Regarding the template, the first section is devoted to cultivating the self overall. It provides ideas on how one may begin to actualize those qualities leading to meaningful, fulfilling lives. The second section is more workplace specific. In this section, we speak to those behaviors we have found important to career success. Ultimately, these are the ideals to which we hope all citizens aspire.

Ten Courageous Choices for Expanding Self

1. **Cultivate and practice honest and open self-reflection**. Honesty with self is the key to accepting responsibility for one's choices and their consequences. It's fundamental to all growth, including personal, career, and spiritual. Honesty with self is the basis of and motivation for changes in behaviors and attitudes. It is vital to empowerment.
2. **Identify and articulate your core values**. Learn all you can about what really makes you feel fulfilled, what resonates with your highest purpose, and what truly gives you joy. Write a personal creed that reflects your values, and keep the creed visible to keep you focused on your journey. Prioritize the values that are most important and least important, those that you can and can't live without.
3. **Align your values with all your choices**. Strive to live from the basis of individual principle, that which tells you right from wrong. Ideally, all your choices would echo your core beliefs/ values. Times may occur when you must reach a "compromised" decision; if this does happen, make sure you're compromising for the right reasons rather than compromising your ethics or integrity.
4. **Focus on positive goals**. Optimism breeds strength and hope, both essential for self-efficacy. A positive attitude is contagious; remaining sanguine despite setbacks is beneficial to both self and others.
5. **Serve your community, however you define community**. Service to community is an integral part of finding and maintaining personal worth. Putting something larger ahead of self is one of the primary components of authentic happiness.

Only through service to others can one know personal well-being.

6. **Seek balance**. Create a harmonious, balanced life that blends family, friends, fun, and light-heartedness with hard work and more serious considerations. Science has shown that "the over-worked, over-achiever" is neither the dream family member nor the ideal employee. Slow down and grow some flowers. The small things, the little day-to-day choices, make the biggest differences in quality of life.

7. **Take the time to learn about others**. Remember the "new golden rule"—do unto others as they would have you do unto them. Practice kindness toward all and embrace diversity. Ultimately, we are defined not by what stuff we have, but by the relationships we've made.

8. **Learn and practice democratic principles**. Despite democracy's flaws, it's still the best governing philosophy the world knows. Remember its true intent, namely, the supreme power is vested in the people. This also means that we must insist on freedom, justice, and social equality for all, which implies that we practice our civic responsibilities conscientiously.

9. **Model global citizenry**. We must set aside all superficial differences (e.g., racial) and work to resolve real differences to everyone's mutual satisfaction. Let's not insist on uniformity across the globe; rather let's seek commonly agreed upon standards of behavior based on trust, respect, integrity, and morality.

10. **Live in a manner that would make your grandmother and your children proud**. When all else fails, apply this test— "Would my grandmother be proud of who I am?"

This next section focuses on attitudes and behaviors for workplace and career success. They can be worked on concomitantly with the preceding suggestions.

Five Courageous Choices for Expanding Career Success

1. **Cultivate Kelley's (1998) STAR behaviors**. They will serve you well not only in the workplace, but also throughout all aspects of your life. They encapsulate much of what we describe as the "Knowledge Nomad."
2. **Capitalize on your strengths**. Using your unique strengths in your job adds immeasurably to your satisfaction levels. Moreover, encourage others to develop theirs. Helping everyone to be the best they can be fosters creativity and innovation. Keep the larger organizational goals and vision uppermost in mind when accomplishing a task. Replace ego with humility, and let circumstances determine who will lead and who will follow.
3. **Make room for others on the ladder of success**. Success is not achieved in isolation, and such a belief is utter arrogance. Many others, knowingly and unknowingly, have helped you become who and what you are. No one feels any lasting sense of internal peace or happiness when success has been attained at the expense of others.
4. **Ask for and give help**. Decisions are better when others have input. Expand human networks to reap the benefits of others' experiences. Real wisdom almost always comes from others. Giving help keeps the spirit of selflessness alive. It builds camaraderie, perpetuates trust, and strengthens relationships.
5. **Continue to learn**. Create learning opportunities and take advantage of those presented to you. Ongoing learning is essential to keeping your career energized as well as your life vital and dynamic.

Above all, we recommend everyone be courageous. Confront your fears about risk and change. Explore new possibilities. Make the hard choices. Climb the tallest peaks. Look behind the shadows and listen to those without voices. Live life fully.

As career development matures and reaches its potential in influencing a new social contract, we believe that professionals leading the charge will find considerable rewards from their efforts. As the Apple Computer ad says, "Those crazy enough to think they can change the world are the one's who do." We wish you well in your "crazy," passionate pursuit of helping students and clients make courageous career choices.

Courageous Questions

Following are ten questions probing how you make choices. Do the choices you make demonstrate courageousness? Asking yourself these "Courageous Questions" can facilitate your becoming a courageous person in your decisions and actions. They can assist you to create a courageous life!

1. What do I need to cultivate within myself to ensure that I take responsibility for creating my life?

2. What are my core values and how do I demonstrate them?

3. How can I align my values with my career goals to find significance in all that I do?

4. How can I best serve my family? My community? My country? My world?

5. How can I be more honoring of others in all that I do?

6. What am I willing to give up to make time for reflection?

7. In my workplace, do I go beyond my expected role to find value-added ideas and encourage the same in others?

8. Do I confront what I need to learn and seek "guru networks" to help me? Do I give help in return?

9. Do I navigate competing interests to promote cooperation and to help move beyond conflict to "getting things done"? Are my motives true to the goals of the organization?

10. Do I act in ways that would make my grandmother and children proud?

"If your life works, you influence your family.
If your family works, your family influences the community.
If your community works, your community influences the nation.
If your nation works, your nation influences the world.
If your world works, the ripple effect spreads throughout the cosmos.
All growth spreads outward from a fertile and potent nucleus. You are a nucleus."

John Heider
The Tao of Leadership, (1985, p. 107).

References

America's Career Resource Network Association. (2003). *The educational, social, and economic value of informed and considered career decisions.* North Dakota: Author.

Amundson, N. E. (2003). *Active engagement: Enhancing the career counseling process.* Richmond, British Columbia, Canada: Ergon Communications.

Anthes, K. (2002). *No Child Left Behind policy brief: School and district leadership.* Denver, CO: Educational Commission of the States. Retrieved July 12, 2004, from http://www.ccsso.org/federal_programs/NCLB/index.cfm

Azrin, N. H., & Besalel, V. A. (1980). *Job club counselor's manual.* Baltimore, MD: University Park Press.

Barry, B. (2001). *The real game series* (Rev. ed). St. John's, Newfoundland, Canada: The Real Game.

Becker, B. E., Huseld, M. S., & Ulrich, D. (2001). *The HR scoreboard: Linking people, strategy, and performance.* Cambridge, MA: Harvard Business School Press.

Bhagwati, J. (2004). *In defense of globalization.* New York: Oxford University Press.

BlessingWhite. (2004). *The organizational dance card: A BlessingWhite survey report on employee engagement.* Princeton, NJ: BlessingWhite, Inc.

Bloom, J. W., & Walz, G. R. (2000). *Cybercounseling and cyberlearning: Strategies and resources for the millennium.* Alexandria, VA: American Counseling Association.

Bloom, J. W., & Walz, G. R. (2004). *Cybercounseling and cyberlearning: An encore.* Greensboro, NC: CAPS Press.

Bolles, R. (1972). *What color is your parachute?* Berkeley, CA: Ten Speed Press.

Bordin, E. S. (1979). The generalizability of the working alliance. *Psychotherapy: Theory, Research and Practice, 16*, 252-260.

Bottoms, G., & Presson, A. (2000). *Using lessons learned: Improving the academic achievement of vocational students.* Educational Benchmarks 2000 Series. Atlanta, GA: Southern Regional Education Board. (ERIC Document Reproduction Service No. ED451366)

Bottoms, G. (2003). *Leading school reform.* Web cast September 4, 2003. Retrieved August 8, 2004, from http://www.nccte.org/webcasts/index.asp?display=archive

Boyatzis, R., McKee, A., & Goleman, D. (2002, April). Reawakening your passion for work. *Harvard Business Review, 80*(4), 86-94.

Buckingham, M., & Clifton, D.O. (2001). *Now discover your strengths.* New York: Free Press.

Business: The ultimate resource. (2002). Cambridge, MA: Perseus Publishing.

Caine, G., & Caine, R. N. (2001). *The brain, education, and the competitive edge.* Lanham, MD: Scarecrow Press, Inc.

Carnevale, A. P. (2004). *What will work be like in the next decade?* Web cast March 4, 2004. Retrieved September 16, 2004, from http://www.nccte.org/webcasts/ description.asp?wc=103

Carnevale, A. P., & Desrochers, D. M. (2003). Preparing students for the knowledge economy: What school counselors need to know. *Professional School Counseling, 6*(4), 228-237.

Charland, B. (1993). *Career shifting: Starting over in a changing economy.* Holbrook, MA: Adams.

Chung, Y. B., & Gfroerer, M. C. (2003). Career coaching: Practice, training, professional, and legal issues. *The Career Development Quarterly, 52*, 141-152.

Clifton, D. O., & Anderson, E. (2002). *Strengths Quest: Discover and develop your strengths in academics, career, and beyond.* Washington, DC: The Gallup Organization.

Clifton, C., & Gonzalez-Molina, G. (2002). *Follow this path: How the world's greatest organizations drive growth by utilizing human potential*. New York: Warner Books.

Coach University. (1999). *Coaching University electronic media kit*. Retrieved September 7, 1999, from http://www.mediakit@coachu.com (No longer accessible. Document available from Y. Barry Chung: bchung@gsu.edu)

Comer, J. P. (2002). Waiting for a miracle: Why schools can't solve our problems and how we can [Electronic version]. *Urban Education Journal*. Retrieved online November 6, 2002, from http://www.urbanedjournal.org/articles/article0002.html

Cromie, W. J. (2001, June 7). How to be happy and well rather than sad and sick [Electronic version]. *Harvard University Gazette*. Retrieved September 15, 2004 from http://www.news.harvard.edu/gazette/2001/06.07/01-happywell.html

Csikszentmihalyi, M. (1991). *Flow*. New York: Harper and Row.

Cuban, L. (1993). *How teachers taught: Constancy and change in American classrooms* (2nd ed.). New York: Teachers College Press.

Daggett, W. R. (2003a). *Why No Child Left Behind matters*. Retrieved July 13, 2004, from http://www.daggett.com/white_papers.html

Daggett, W. R. (2003b). *Jobs and the skills gap*. Retrieved July 13, 2004, from http://www.daggett.com/white_papers.html

Daggett, W. R. (2003c). School counselors and information literacy from the perspective of Willard Daggett. *Professional School Counseling, 6*(4), 238-243.

Daggett, W. R. (2004a). Academic and technical skills for the 21st century. Web cast May 6, 2004. Retrieved August 8, 2004, from http://www.nccte.org/webcasts/index.asp?display=archive

Daggett, W. R. (2004b). *America's most successful high schools—What makes them work*. Rexford, NY: International Center for Leadership in Education.

Dawis, R. V. (1984). Job satisfaction: Worker's aspiration, attitudes and behavior. In N. C. Gysbers (Ed.), *Designing career counseling to enhance education, work and leisure*. San Francisco: Jossey-Bass.

DePree, M. (1997). *Leading without power: Finding hope in serving community*. San Francisco, CA: Jossey-Bass, Inc.

Derr, C. B. (1986). *Managing the new careerists*. San Francisco, CA: Jossey-Bass.

deSoto, H. (2004). *The mystery of capital: Why capitalism triumphs in the west and fails everywhere else*. New York: Basic Books.

Diener, E., & Seligman, M. (2004). Beyond money. *Psychological Science in the Public Interest, 5*(1), 1-31.

Dobbs, L. (2004). *Exporting America: Why corporate greed is shipping American jobs overseas.* New York: Warner Books.

Dominquez, J., & Robin, V. (1992). *Your money or your life*. New York: Penguin Books.

Dossey, L. (1999). *Reinventing medicine: Beyond mind-body to a new era of healing*. San Francisco, CA: Harper.

Drucker, P. (2004, January 12). Peter Drucker sets us straight. *Fortune, 149*(1), 114-118.

Dubois, D. D. (Ed.) (2002-2003, Winter). Competencies from the individual's viewpoint [Special issue]. *Career Planning and Adult Development Journal, 18*(4).

Dychtwald, K. (2000). *Age power: How the 21st century will be ruled by the new old*. New York: Putnam.

Dykeman, C., Herr, E. L., Ingram, M., Wood, C., Charles, S., & Pehrsson, D. (2001). *The taxonomy of career development interventions that occur in America's secondary schools*. Minneapolis, MN: University of Minnesota, National Research Center for Career and Technical Education.

Eckersley, R. (2004, September-October). A new world view struggles to emerge. *The Futurist, 38*(5) 20-25.

Eichinger, R. W., Lombardo, M. M., & Raymond, C. C. (2004). *FYI for talent management*. Minneapolis, MN: Lominger Limited, Inc.

Feller, R. W. (1997). Redefining "career" during the work revolution. In R. W. Feller & G. Walz (Eds.), *Career transitions in turbulent times: Exploring work, learning and careers*. Greensboro, NC: ERIC/CASS Publications.

Feller, R. W. (Ed.) (2003a). Using career assessments with adults [Special issue]. *Career Planning and Adult Development Journal, 19*(2).

Feller, R. W. (2003b). Aligning school counseling, the changing workplace, and career development assumptions. *Professional School Counseling, 6*(4), 262-271.

Feller, R. W., & Davies, T. G. (Eds.) (1999a). Innovative models of teaching career counselors [Special issue]. *Career Planning and Adult Development Journal, 15*(2).

Feller, R. W., & Davies, T. G. (1999b). Career development for all. In Pautler, A. (Ed.), *Workforce education: Issues for the new century*. Ann Arbor, MI: Prakken.

Feller, R. W., & Walz, G. (1997). *Career transitions in turbulent times: Exploring work, learning and careers*. Greensboro, NC: ERIC/CASS Publications.

Ferris State University. (2002). *Decisions without direction: Career guidance and decision-making among American youth*. Ferris State University: Author.

Festinger, L. (1957). *Theory of cognitive dissonance*. Stanford, CA: Stanford University Press.

Figler, H., & Bolles, R. N. (1999). *The career counselor's handbook*. Berkeley, CA: Ten Speed Press.

Friedman, T. L. (2003). American's labor pains. In H. S. Schaffner & C. E. Van Horn (Eds.), *A nation at work* (pp. 203-204). New Brunswick, NJ: Rutgers University Press.

Fogg, N. P., Harrington, P. E., & Harrington, T. F. (2004). *College majors handbook*. Indianapolis, IN: JIST.

Follow Your True Colors. (n.d.). Retrieved October 4, 2004, from http://truecolorscareer.com/

Galinsky, E. (2003). *Duel-Centric: A new concept of work-life*. Retrieved November, 22, 2003, from http://www.familiesandwork.org/summery/duel-centric.pdf

Gallup Organization. (1999). *National survey of Working America*. Princeton, NJ: Author.

Gelatt, H. B. (1998). Positive uncertainty: A new decision making framework for counseling. *Journal of Counseling Psychology, 36*(2).

Gillie, S., & Gillie-Isenhour, M. (2003). *The Educational, Social and Economic Value of Informed and Considered Career Decisions*. Washington, DC: U. S. Department of Education Office of Vocational and Adult Education America's Career Resource Network.

Goldman, D. (1995). *Emotional intelligence*. New York: Bantam Books.

Goldman, D. (1998). *Emotional intelligence at work*. New York: Bantam Books.

Goodlad, J. I. (2002). Kudzu, rabbits, and school reform. *Phi Delta Kappan, 84*(1), 16-23.

Gorman, B. (2003). Employee engagement after two decades of change: Revisiting Roger D'Aprix's Manager's Communication Model 20 years on. *SCM, 7*(1), 14-17.

Grant, A. M. (2002). Towards a psychology of coaching: The impact of coaching on metacognition, mental health and goal attainment. (Doctoral dissertation, Macquarie University, New South Wales, Australia, 2002). *Dissertation Abstracts International, 63/12B*, 6094.

Gray, K. C. (2002). *The role of career and technical education in the American high school: A student centered analysis*. Pittsburgh, PA: Penn State University.

Gray, K. C., & Herr, E. L. (2000). *Other ways to win: Creating alternatives for high school graduates* (2nd ed.). Thousand Oaks, CA: Corwin Press, Inc.

Greenspan's social security alarm. (2004, August 27). *CBSNEWS.com*. Retrieved September 16, 2004, from http://www.cbsnews.com/stories/ 2004/08/27/national/printable638921.shtml

Grubb, W. N. (1996). *Working in the middle*. San Francisco, CA: Jossey-Bass, Inc.

Gysbers, N. C. (2001). School guidance and counseling in the 21st century: Remembering the past into the future. *Professional School Counseling, 65*, 96-105.

Gysbers, N. C., Heppner, M. J., & Johnston, J.A. (2003). *Career counseling: Process, issues, and techniques*. Boston, MA: Allyn and Bacon.

Hansen, L. S. (1997). *Integrative life planning: Critical tasks for career development and changing life patterns*. San Francisco, CA: Jossey-Bass.

Harkins, A. M. (2002). *The future of career and technical education in a continuous innovation society*. Columbus, OH: The Ohio State University, National Career and Technical Teacher Education Institute.

Harrington, T. F. (2003). Career counseling strategies. In T. Harrington (Ed.), *Handbook of career planning for students with special needs* (pp. 77-108). Austin, TX: Pro-Ed.

Hawken, P., Lovins, A., & Lovins, L. H. (1999). *Natural capitalism: Creating the next industrial revolution*. Boston: Little, Brown and Co.

Heet, J. (2004). America and the coming global workforce. *American Outlook, VII*(1), 29-33.

Heider, J. (1985). *Tao of leadership*. Atlanta, GA: Humanics Limited.

Herman, R., Olivo, T., & Gioia, J. (2003). *Impending crisis: Too many jobs, too few people*. Winchester, VA: Oakhill Press.

Herr, E. L. (1999). *Counseling in a dynamic society: Opportunities and challenges*. Alexandria, VA: American Counseling Association.

Herr, E. L., Cramer, S. H., & Niles, S. G. (2004). *Career guidance and counseling through the life span: Systematic approaches* (5th ed.). Boston, MA: Allyn & Bacon.

Hinds, M. (2003). *The triumph of the flexible society*. Westport, CT: Praeger Publishers.

Honoré, C. (2004). *In praise of slowness: How a worldwide movement is challenging the cult of speed*. San Francisco, CA: Harper.

Hornstein, H. A. (2003). *The haves and the have nots: The abuse of power and privilege in the workplace...and how to control it*. Upper Saddle River, NJ: Financial Times Prentice Hall.

Hudson, F. M. (1999). *The handbook of coaching: A comprehensive resource guide for managers, executives, consultants and human resource professionals*. San Francisco, CA: Jossey Bass.

Hughes, K. L., Bailey, T. R., & Karp, M. M. (2002). School-to-work: Making a difference in education. *Phi Delta Kappan, 84*(4), 272-279.

Ibarra, H. (2003). *Working identity: Unconventional strategies for reinventing your career*. Boston, MA: Harvard Business School Press.

Interagency Forum on Child and Family Statistics. (2002). *America's children: Key indicators of well-being*. Retrieved October 2, 2004, from http://www.childstats.gov/ac2002/index.asp

Is your job next? (2003, February 3). *Business Week*, pp. 56-57.

Jarvis, P., Zielke, J., & Cartwright, C. (2003). From career decision making to career management: It's all about lifelong learning. In G. Walz & R. Knowdell, (Eds.), *Global Realities: Celebrating our differences, honoring our connections* (pp. 269-280). Greensboro, NC: CAPS Press.

Jeserich, N., & Toft, G. (2004). The new geography of American jobs. *American Outlook, VII*(1), 25-29.

Johnston, D. (2003). *Perfectly legal: The covert campaign to rig our tax system to benefit the super rich and cheat everybody else*. New York: Penquin Group.

Jones, D. (2001). *Celebrate what's right with the world*. St. Paul, MN: Star Thrower Distribution Corporation.

Kalil, C. (1998). *Follow your true colors to the work you love*. Corona, CA: True Colors.

Kelley, R. E. (1998). *How to be a star at work: Nine breakthrough strategies you need to succeed*. New York: Times Business.

Kerka, S. (2003). Possible selves: Envisioning the future. *Trends and Issues Alert, 48*. Retrieved October 2, 2004, from http://www.cete.org/acve/docgen.asp?tbl=tia&ID=171

Kirkegaard, J. F. (2004). Outsourcing—Stains on the white collar? Retrieved October 2, 2004, from http://www.stern.nyu.edu/globalmacro/cur_policy/outsourcing.html

Kohn, A. (1999). *The schools our children deserve: Moving beyond traditional classrooms and "tougher standards"*. New York: Houghton Mifflin Company.

Kolb, D. A. (1984). *Experiential learning: Experience as the source of learning and development*. Englewood Cliffs, NJ: Prentice Hall.

Krumboltz, J. D., & Levin A. S. (2004). *Luck is no accident—Making the most of happenstance in your life and work*. Atascadero, CA: Impact Publishers.

Lamb, G. M. (2004, August 30). Coming soon: Robo-greeter [Electronic version]. *The Christian Science Monitor*. Retrieved September 16, 2004, from http://www.csmonitor.com/2004/0830/p13s01-wmgm.htm.

Lawson, E., & Price, C. (2003). The psychology of change management. *The McKinsey Quarterly*. Available from http:www.mckinseyquarterly.com/.

Levy, F., & Murnane, R. J. (2004). *The new division of labor: How computers are creating the next job market*. Princeton, NJ: Princeton University Press.

Lewis, A. C. (2004, August). Rethinking the American high school. *TechDirections*, 5-6.

Lohr, S. (2004, September 9). An elder challenges outsourcing's orthodoxy [Electronic version]. *The New York Times*. Retrieved September 9, 2004 from http://www.nytimes.com.

Lombardo, M., & Eichinger, R. W. (2002a). *The career architect development planner*. Minneapolis, MN: Lominger.

Lombardo, M. W., & Eichinger, R. W. (2002b). *The leadership machine: Architecture to developing leaders for any future*. Minneapolis, MN: Lominger.

Lowman, R. (1996). Who will help us work more functionally? In R. Feller & G. Walz. (Eds.), *Career transitions in turbulent times: Exploring work, learning and careers* (pp. 205-210). Greensboro, NC: ERIC/CASS.

Marklein, M. B. (2004, August 5). The 'major' dilemma: To those parents obsessed with where their school-age son or daughter will go to college, a trio of Northeastern University professors suggests a redirection of energy. *USA Today*. p. D.06.

Markus, H., & Nurius, P. (1986). Possible selves. *American Psychologist, 41*, 954-969.

Meier, D. (2002). Standardization versus standards. *Phi Delta Kappan, 84*(3), 190-198.

Michaels, E., Handfield-Jones, H., & Axelrod, B. (2001). *The war for talent*. Boston, MA: Harvard Business School Press.

Miscisin, M. (2001). *Showing our true colors*. Riverside, CA: True Colors Publishing.

Mishel, L., Berstein, J., & Allegretto, S. (2003). *The state of working America 2004-05*. Retrieved September 15, 2004, from http://www.epinet.org

Montgomery, R., & Palmer, E. (2004, April 4). A giant muscles in: China's hot economy puts pressure on U.S. *The Kansas City Star*, pp. A1, A10.

Murphy, J. J. (1999). Common factors of school-based change. In M. A. Hubble, B. L. Duncan, & S. D. Miller (Eds.), *The heart & soul of change: What works in therapy* (pp. 361-288). Washington, DC: American Psychological Association.

Myers, I. B., & McCaulley, M. H. (1985). *Manual: A guide to the development and use of the Myers-Briggs Type Indicator.* Palo Alto, CA: Consulting Psychologists Press.

National Association of Secondary School Principals. (2004). Breaking Ranks II: Strategies for leading high school reform. Retrieved July 27, 2004, from http://www.nassp.org/breakingranks/ breakingranks2.cfm

National Life/Work Centre, Canada Career Information Partnership, & Human Resources Development Canada. (n.d.) *Blueprint for Life/ Work Designs.* Retrieved January 7, 2004, from http://www. blueprint4life.ca

National Occupational Information Coordinating Committee (NOICC). (1996). *National career development guidelines: K-adult handbook.* Stillwater, OK: NOICC Training Support Center.

Niles, S. G., & Pate, P. H. (1989). Competency and training issues related to the integration of career counseling and mental health counseling. *Journal of Career Development, 16,* 63-71.

No Child Left Behind Act of 2001. H.R. 1, 107th Cong. (2001).

Nordgren, R.D. (2002). Globalization and education: What students will need to know and be able to do in the global village. *Phi Delta Kappan, 84*(4), 318-321.

Palmore, E. (1969). Predicting longevity: A follow-up controlling for age. *Gerontologist, 9,* 247-250.

Parnell, D. (1996). Cerebral context. *Vocational Education Journal, 71*(3), 18-21.

Pfeffer, J. (2004, August). All work, no play? It doesn't pay. *Business 2.0, 5*(7), 50.

Pink, D. (2001). *Free agent nation: The future of working for yourself.* New York: Warner Books.

Plank, S. (2001). *Career and technical education in the balance: An analysis of high school persistence, academic achievement, and postsecondary destinations.* Report from Columbus, OH: The Ohio State University, National Dissemination Center for Career and Technical Education.

Posner, D. (2002). Education for the 21st Century. *Phi Delta Kappan, 84*(4), 316-317.

Prochaska, J. O. (2003). How do people change, and how can we change to help many more people? In M. Hubble, B.L Duncan, & S. Miller (Eds.), *The heart & soul of change* (pp. 227-258). Washington, DC: American Psychological Association.

Rath, T., & Clifton, D. O. (2004). *How full is your bucket?* New York: Gallup Press.

Reich, R. B. (1992). *The work of nations: Preparing ourselves for 21st-century capitalism.* New York: Vintage Books.

Reich, R. B. (2002). *I'll be short: Essential for a decent working society.* New York: Alfred A. Knopf.

Reich, R. B. (2004). *Reason: Why liberals will win the battle for America.* New York: Alfred A. Knopf.

Renzulli, J. S. (2002). Expanding the conception of giftedness to include co-cognitive traits and to promote social capital. *Phi Delta Kappan, 84*(1), 33-58.

Rockport Institute. (2003). An interview with Rockport founder Nicholas Lore about career fit and satisfaction. Retrieved Jan. 7, 2004, from http://rockportinstitute.com

Rodrik, D. (1997). *Has globalization gone too far?* Washington, DC: Institute for International Economics.

Rogers, F. (2003). *The world according to Mister Rogers.* New York: Hyperion.

Rosenbaum, J. E., & Person, A. E. (2003). Beyond college for all: Policies and practices to improve transitions into college and jobs. *Professional School Counseling, 64*, 252-260.

Satin, M. (2004). *Radical middle: The politics we need now.* Boulder, CO: Westview Press.

Savickas, M. L. (1992). New directions in career assessment. In D. H. Montross & C. J. Shinkman (Eds.), *Career development* (pp. 336-355). Springfield, IL: Charles C. Thomas.

Savickas, M. L. (2000). Career development and public policy: The role of values, theory and research. In B. Hiebert & L. Bezanson, (Eds.), *Making waves: Career development and public policy: International Symposium 1999 Papers, Proceedings and Strategies* (pp. 52-68). Ottawa, Canada: Canadian Career Development Foundation.

Savickas, M. L. (2003). Career counseling in the next decade [Special issue]. *The Career Development Quarterly, 52*(1).

Schaffner, H. A., & Van Horn, C. E. (2003). Social, economic and demographic trends. In H. A. Schaffner & C. E. Van Horn (Eds.), *A nation at work* (pp. 3-66). Piscataway, NJ: Rutgers University Press.

Schwartz, B. (2004, January 23). The tyranny of choice [Electronic version]. *The Chronicle of Higher Education, 50*(20). Retrieved August 18, 2004, from http://chronicle.come/weekly/v50/i20/20b00601.htm

Search Institute. (1997). *The asset approach: giving kids what they need to succeed.* Minneapolis, MN: Author.

Seligman, M. E. (2002). *Authentic happiness: Using the new positive psychology to realize your potential for lasting fulfillment.* New York: The Free Press.

Silva, P. (2004). An authentic test for our children: Ten common principles in a time of grief. *Phi Delta Kappan, 85*(4), 707-708.

Simonsen, P. (1997). *Promoting a development culture in your organization: Using career development as a change agent.* Palo Alto, CA: Davies-Black.

Snitow, A. (Director), & Kaufman, D. (Director). (2001). *Secrets of Silicon Valley* [Video recording]. (Available from Bullfrog Films, P.O. Box 149, Oley, PA 19547)

Snyder, C. R., Feldman, D. B., Shorey, H. S. & Rand, K. L. (2002). Hopeful choices: A school counselor's guide to the hope theory. *Professional School Counseling, 5*(5), 298-307.

Snyder, D. P. (2004, July-August). Five meta-trends changing the world. *The Futurist*, 22-27.

Steinberg, A., & Allen, L. (2002). *From large to small: Strategies for personalizing the high school*. Boston, MA: Jobs for the Future.

Steinberg, A., & Cohen, M. (2002, March 13). Rigor and relevance. *Education Week, XXI*(26).

Steinberg, L. (1996). *Beyond the classroom: Why school reform has failed and what parents need to do*. New York: Touchstone.

Stephens, G. (2002). Can we create a kinder, gentler world (or at least a safe one)? A twelve-step program. Retrieved August 18, 2004, from http://www.wfs.org/stephens.htm

Stewart, T. A. (2001). *The wealth of knowledge: Intellectual capital and the twenty-first century organization*. New York: Doubleday.

Stewart, T. (2002, November). How to think with your gut [Electronic version]. *Business 2.0, 3*(11).

Symonds, W. C. (2002, October 14). Closing the school gap. *Business Week, 3803*, 124-125.

Thornburg, D. (2002). *The new basics: Education and the future of work in the telematic age*. Alexandria, VA: Association for Supervision and Curriculum Development.

Thurow, L. C. (1999). *Building wealth: The new rules for individuals, companies, and nations in a knowledge-based economy*. New York: Harper Collins.

Training for jobs. (1994, March 12). *The Economist, 330*(7584), pp. 19-20, 26.

True Colors Inc. (2003). *True Colors Communication Group*. Retrieved October 4, 2004, from http://www.true-colors.com/about/index.htm

U. S. Department of Commerce. (2002). Census bureau report shows "big payoff" from educational degrees [Electronic version].

U.S. Department of Commerce News. Retrieved August 17, 2004, from http://www.census.gov/Press-Release /www/2002/cb02-95.html

U. S. Department of Commerce. (2003). Information technology and the new economy. In H. S. Schaffner & C. E. Van Horn (Eds.), *A nation at work* (pp. 129-132). New Brunswick, NJ: Rutgers University Press.

U. S. Department of Labor, Bureau of Labor Statistics. (2002). *Working in the 21st Century*. Retrieved December 31, 2002, from http://www.bls.gov/opub/working/home.htm

U. S. Department of Labor, Bureau of Labor Statistics. (2004). Number of jobs held in a lifetime [Electronic version]. *Bureau of Labor Statistics News*. Retrieved September 4, 2004, from http://www.bls.gov/nls

Useem, M. (2004, September). Can you prepare to be courageous? *Fortune, (86)*, 99.

Wakefield, S. M., Sage, H., Coy, D. R., & Palmer, T. (Eds.). (2004). *Unfocused kids: Helping students to focus on their education and career plans*. Greensboro, NC: CAPS Press.

Walz, G. R., Miller, R., & Malone, J. (in press). *Distance counseling: A handbook for educators and practitioners*. Austin, TX: Pro-Ed, Inc.

Warshaw, M. (1998, June-July). Get a life [Electronic version]. *Fast Company (15)*, 138. Retrieved October 2, 2004, from http://www.fastcompany.com/online/15/getalife.html

Watts, A. G. , Dartois, C., & Plant, P. (1986). *Educational and vocational guidance services for the 14-25 age group in the European Community*. Brussels, Belgium: Commission of the European Communities, Directorate-General for Employment, Social Affairs and Education.

Watts, A. G. (1996). The changing concept of career: Implications for career counseling. In R. Feller & G. Walz. (Eds.), *Career transitions in turbulent times: Exploring work, learning and careers* (pp. 229-235). Greensboro, NC: ERIC/CASS.

Whitmyer, C. (1994). *Mindfulness and meaningful work.* Berkeley, CA: Parallex Press.

Whitworth, L., Kimsey-House, H., & Sandahl, P. (1998). *Co-active coaching: New skills for coaching people toward success in work and life.* Palo-Alto, CA: Davies-Black.

Wonacott, M. E. (2002a). *The impact of work-based learning on students.* Columbus, OH: The Ohio State University, ERIC Clearinghouse on Adult, Career and Vocational Education. (ERIC Digest No. 242)

Wonacott, M. E. (2002b). *Dropouts and career and technical education.* Columbus, OH: The Ohio State University, National Career and Technical Teacher Education Institute.

Yankelovich, D. (1999). *That magic of dialogue.* New York: Touchstone.

Yergin, D., & Stanislaw, J. (2002). *The commanding heights: The battle for the world economy.* New York, NY: Touchstone.